The Principle Book

By Daniel Melehi

©December 2023

Contents

Introduction

Welcome to "The Principle Book 80 Business Principles Every Entrepreneur Must Know." In this book, we will explore the fundamental principles and laws that govern the business world. Whether you are a seasoned entrepreneur or just starting your own business, understanding these rules is crucial for your success. Businesses operate in complex and ever-changing environments. To thrive amidst competition, business owners need to make informed decisions and implement effective strategies. The key to achieving this lies in comprehending and leveraging the principles and laws that have stood the test of time. In this book, we will dive into a wide range of topics, including marketing, leadership, customer service, financial management, decision-making, and much more. Each chapter will explore a specific business rule or law, providing you with practical insights and actionable advice. As you read through the chapters, you will gain a deeper understanding of the principles that drive business success. You will learn how to apply these rules to overcome challenges, seize opportunities, and build a thriving and sustainable business. It is important to note that these rules are not meant to be rigid guidelines but rather tools for smart decision-making. While they provide valuable frameworks, successful business owners also know when and how to adapt them to suit their unique circumstances. Throughout the book, you will find real-life examples and case studies that illustrate the application of these rules in various business contexts. Learning from the experiences of other successful entrepreneurs and professionals will give you a practical perspective on how to implement these principles effectively. Remember, knowledge without action is meaningless. To truly benefit from this book, it is essential to reflect on each rule and consider how you can apply it to your own business. Take the time to evaluate your current strategies and practices, and identify areas where these rules can help you improve. By the time you finish reading "The Principle Book 80 Business Principles Every Entrepreneur Must Know," you will be equipped with a comprehensive toolkit of principles and laws that can guide you towards business success. Let's embark on this journey of exploration and discovery together.

ACKNOWLEDGMENTS

Before we dive into the chapters, I want to express my gratitude to all the experts, business leaders, and authors whose work has influenced and shaped this book. Their wisdom and insights have contributed to the compilation of these essential business rules. I would also like to acknowledge the support and encouragement of my family and friends throughout the writing process. Their unwavering belief in my abilities has been instrumental in completing this book. Lastly, I want to extend my heartfelt gratitude to you, the reader. I hope the knowledge and advice shared in this book will empower you to take your business to new heights. May these 80 business rules serve as beacons of guidance as you navigate the dynamic and challenging landscape of entrepreneurship. Now, let's begin our journey into the world of business rules and their impact on your success.

Chapter 1: The 80/20 Rule

Chapter 1: The 80/20 Rule

The 80/20 rule, also known as the Pareto Principle, is a fundamental concept in business that states that 80% of the outcomes or results are derived from 20% of the inputs or efforts. This principle was named after Italian economist Vilfredo Pareto, who observed that 80% of the land in Italy was owned by 20% of the population. In the context of business, the 80/20 rule implies that a significant portion of a company's success comes from a small fraction of its activities, products, or customers. By understanding and leveraging this principle, business owners can prioritize their efforts and resources to focus on the most productive and profitable areas. One application of the 80/20 rule is customer segmentation. By analyzing customer data, businesses can identify the top 20% of their customers who generate the majority of their revenue. They can then tailor their marketing strategies and customer service initiatives to cater to this segment, maximizing their return on investment. Another aspect of the 80/20 rule is resource allocation. Business owners should identify the key activities or projects that contribute the most to their bottom line and allocate their resources accordingly. By focusing on the vital few, they can optimize their productivity and efficiency. However, it's important to note that the 80/20 rule is not a strict formula but rather a general guideline. The percentages may vary in different situations, but the underlying principle remains the same – a small portion of efforts or inputs generates the majority of results. By embracing the 80/20 rule, business owners can streamline their operations, increase profitability, and make better decisions regarding resource allocation. It encourages them to identify the most valuable aspects of their business and invest their time, money, and energy wisely.

Key Takeaways:

- The 80/20 rule, or the Pareto Principle, states that 80% of results come from 20% of efforts. - Businesses can use the 80/20 rule to identify their most valuable customers, products, or activities. - Resource allocation should be based on the vital few areas that generate the majority of results. - The 80/20 rule is a guideline and may vary in different situations. - By leveraging the 80/20 rule, businesses can optimize productivity and make better decisions.

Chapter 2: The Pareto Principle

The Pareto Principle, also known as the 80/20 rule, is a concept that states that roughly 80% of the effects come from 20% of the causes. This rule was named after the Italian economist Vilfredo Pareto, who observed that 80% of the land in Italy was owned by 20% of the population. In the business world, the Pareto Principle can be applied in various ways to prioritize efforts and resources. By understanding this principle, business owners can make better decisions and achieve greater results. One application of the Pareto Principle is in customer segmentation. By analyzing customer data, business owners can identify the top 20% of customers who generate the most revenue. These customers are often referred to as "high-value" or "VIP" customers. By focusing on this segment, businesses can allocate their resources more effectively, ensuring that they meet the needs of their most valuable customers. Another way to apply the Pareto Principle is in resource allocation. By identifying the key activities or projects that contribute the most to the bottom line, business owners can prioritize their efforts and allocate their resources accordingly. This allows them to focus on the activities that have the greatest impact on their business and eliminate or reduce the resources invested in less significant activities. It is important to note that the 80/20 rule is a general guideline and may vary in different situations. The specific percentages may not always be exactly 80% and 20%, but the principle remains the same – a small portion of efforts or inputs often leads to a large portion of results or outputs. By embracing the Pareto Principle, business owners can streamline operations, increase profitability, and make better decisions. It allows them to identify the key areas where they should focus their efforts and resources, maximizing their impact and achieving greater success. In conclusion, the Pareto Principle, or the 80/20 rule, is a powerful concept that can be applied in business to prioritize efforts and resources. By understanding this principle and applying it to customer segmentation and resource allocation, business owners can achieve better results and increase their overall efficiency.

Chapter 3: The Law of Supply and Demand

The Law of Supply and Demand is a fundamental concept in economics that plays a crucial role in determining prices in market economies. It states that the price of a product or service is determined by the relationship between the quantity of that product or service available (supply) and the level of consumer desire for it (demand).

UNDERSTANDING SUPPLY

Supply refers to the amount of a product or service that producers are willing and able to offer for sale at a given price level. It is influenced by various factors, including production costs, technology, availability of resources, government policies, and the number of producers in the market. The law of supply states that as the price of a product or service increases, the quantity supplied by producers also increases, and vice versa. This relationship is known as the supply curve, which is typically upward sloping. Producers are motivated by profit, and when prices are high, it becomes more attractive for them to allocate resources to produce and supply more goods or services. Conversely, when prices are low, producers have less incentive to supply as the profitability of producing the product becomes limited.

UNDERSTANDING DEMAND

Demand, on the other hand, refers to the quantity of a product or service that consumers are willing and able to purchase at a given price level. It is influenced by factors such as consumer preferences, income levels, population demographics, marketing efforts, and the availability of substitute products. The law of demand states that as the price of a product or service increases, the quantity demanded by consumers decreases, and vice versa. This relationship is typically represented by a downward sloping demand curve. When prices are high, consumers may seek alternative products or reduce their consumption, leading to a decrease in the quantity demanded. Conversely, when prices are low, consumers are more willing to purchase the product, leading to an increase in demand.

EQUILIBRIUM PRICE AND QUANTITY

The law of supply and demand dictates that an equilibrium price and quantity will be established in a market where the supply and demand curves intersect. This equilibrium point represents the most efficient allocation of resources and maximizes the overall welfare of both consumers and producers. When the price is above the equilibrium level, there is excess supply, and producers may need to lower prices to sell their surplus. Conversely, when the price is below the equilibrium level, there is excess demand, and producers may increase prices to capture additional profit.

IMPLICATIONS FOR BUSINESS

Understanding the law of supply and demand is essential for business owners and managers as it directly impacts pricing strategies, production decisions, and market positioning. By analyzing market trends, consumer behavior, and competitor actions, businesses can adjust their supply to align with demand and set optimal prices. They can anticipate shifts in demand and adjust production levels accordingly to avoid excess inventory or stockouts. Businesses can also leverage the law of supply and demand to identify opportunities for growth. By identifying niche markets or segments with high demand and limited supply, businesses can develop unique products or services that can command premium prices. Furthermore, businesses can use the law of supply and demand to formulate effective marketing and sales strategies. By understanding consumer preferences and the price elasticity of demand, businesses can adjust pricing, promotions, and distribution to maximize their market share and profitability.

CONCLUSION

The law of supply and demand is a fundamental principle that governs market economies. It highlights the relationship between supply and demand and the resulting impact on prices. By understanding and leveraging this principle, businesses can make informed decisions, optimize resource allocation, and achieve sustainable growth in competitive markets.

Chapter 4: The Rule of Three

The Rule of Three is a principle that suggests that things presented in groups of three are more appealing, memorable, and effective than other numbers. This rule has been widely used in various fields, including business, marketing, and public speaking. By understanding and harnessing the power of the Rule of Three, business owners can enhance their communication, engage their audience, and achieve better results.

WHY THREE?

The human brain is wired to process information in patterns and structures. The number three is considered a magical number in terms of cognition and memory. It is easier for our brain to remember and process information when presented in groups of three. This is commonly referred to as the "triads" phenomenon.

APPLICATION IN BUSINESS

In business, the Rule of Three can be applied in various ways to enhance communication, marketing messages, and decision-making. Here are some examples:

1. Marketing and Advertising

When designing marketing campaigns or advertisements, using the Rule of Three can make the message more memorable and persuasive. A slogan with three words or phrases has a better chance of sticking in people's minds. For example, the popular advertising slogan "Just Do It" by Nike is simple, impactful, and easy to remember.

2. Product or Service Offerings

Presenting product or service offerings in groups of three can help consumers make decisions more easily. Offering three pricing options or three different product bundles gives customers a sense of choice without overwhelming them with too many options. This strategy is commonly used in menu design, where restaurants often present three options for appetizers, entrees, and desserts.

3. Presentations and Public Speaking

When delivering presentations or engaging in public speaking, structuring your content around three main points or themes can make it more concise and memorable. This approach helps the audience follow and retain information more effectively. This technique is commonly used in TED Talks and keynote speeches to keep the audience engaged and focused.

STORYTELLING AND THE POWER OF THREE

The Rule of Three is also prevalent in storytelling and narratives. Stories often follow a three-act structure, where the setup, confrontation, and resolution are the main components. Using the Rule of Three in storytelling can create a satisfying narrative arc and keep the audience engaged. Additionally, in persuasive communication, using three examples or testimonials to support an argument can make it more compelling and persuasive. People tend to remember and relate better to stories or examples presented in threes.

CAUTIONARY NOTES

While the Rule of Three can be a powerful tool, it is important to use it judiciously. Overusing the rule or trying too hard to fit everything into groups of three can come across as contrived or cliché. It is best to use the Rule of Three when it naturally enhances the message or content, rather than as a forced structure.

CONCLUSION

The Rule of Three is a powerful principle in communication, marketing, and decision-making. By understanding its influence on human cognition and memory, business owners can leverage this principle to make their messages more memorable, engaging, and persuasive. Whether it is in marketing slogans, product offerings, presentations, or storytelling, the Rule of Three can help businesses stand out, connect with their audience, and achieve their desired outcomes.

Chapter 5: The Law of Diminishing Returns

The Law of Diminishing Returns is an economic concept that states that as more resources are allocated to a specific activity, the incremental output or benefit derived from each additional unit of input will eventually start to decline. In other words, there comes a point when the added input or effort does not proportionally increase the desired output. This law is based on the observation that in the initial stages, increasing the quantity of a variable input, such as labor or capital, leads to a corresponding increase in output. However, as the input continues to increase beyond a certain point, the additional output gained diminishes and may even become negative. Business owners and managers must recognize and understand the Law of Diminishing Returns as it has important implications for resource allocation and decision-making. Here are some key points to consider:

1. OPTIMAL RESOURCE ALLOCATION:

To achieve maximum efficiency and output, businesses need to determine the ideal level of inputs for a given activity. This means finding the optimal balance between input and output, where the marginal benefit equals the marginal cost. As the law of diminishing returns sets in, allocating additional resources beyond this optimal level can lead to wasted resources and decreased productivity.

2. PRODUCTIVITY AND COSTS:

The Law of Diminishing Returns suggests that as more resources are allocated to a specific activity, the cost per unit of output increases. For example, in manufacturing, adding more workers beyond a certain point may lead to congested workspaces, coordination issues, and decreased production efficiency, ultimately driving up costs.

Businesses need to carefully analyze their production processes and identify the optimal point where costs are minimized and productivity is maximized.

3. TIME MANAGEMENT:

The concept of diminishing returns also applies to time management. Spending excessive time on a particular task may initially bring about significant improvements. However, dedicating too much time beyond a certain point may result in diminishing returns. It is crucial to prioritize tasks and allocate time effectively to ensure that efforts are focused on the most valuable activities.

4. DECISION MAKING AND INNOVATION:

Understanding the Law of Diminishing Returns can help business owners make informed decisions regarding resource allocation and innovation. It encourages them to critically evaluate the potential benefits and drawbacks of increasing inputs, as well as explore alternative approaches that may yield better returns. By strategically allocating resources and exploring innovative solutions, businesses can overcome the challenges posed by diminishing returns.

5. CONTINUOUS IMPROVEMENT:

To mitigate the effects of diminishing returns, businesses should focus on continuous improvement. This involves regularly assessing and optimizing processes, identifying bottlenecks, and implementing strategies to enhance productivity and efficiency. By embracing a culture of continuous improvement, businesses can continually find ways to overcome diminishing returns and drive sustainable growth. In conclusion, the Law of Diminishing Returns highlights the importance of optimizing resource allocation and managing productivity in business. By recognizing the point of diminishing returns, business owners can make informed decisions, manage costs, and focus on strategies that deliver the most significant impact. Embracing a mindset of continuous improvement enables businesses to overcome the challenges imposed by diminishing returns and remain competitive in the ever-changing business landscape. Next, let's dive into Chapter 6: The Rule of Reciprocity.

Chapter 6: The Rule of Reciprocity

Reciprocity is a powerful social and psychological principle that plays a significant role in business relationships and interactions. The Rule of Reciprocity states that when someone does something nice for us, we feel obligated to return the favor. This concept has profound implications for businesses seeking to build strong customer relationships, establish partnerships, and foster loyalty. In the world of business, reciprocity can be observed in various ways. For example, providing exceptional customer service often leads to customers feeling grateful and more likely to make repeat purchases or recommend the business to others. Similarly, when a company gives out free samples or offers a trial period for their products or services, customers often feel compelled to reciprocate by making a purchase or subscribing. By understanding the Rule of Reciprocity, businesses can leverage this principle to their advantage. Here are some key strategies to apply this rule effectively:

1. PROVIDE VALUE

To elicit reciprocity from customers, it is crucial to consistently provide them with value. This can be in the form of high-quality products or services, personalized experiences, timely and efficient customer support, or valuable resources such as educational content. When customers perceive that they have received value from a business, they are more likely to reciprocate by making a purchase or engaging in positive word-of-mouth.

2. SURPRISE AND DELIGHT

Going above and beyond customer expectations can create a sense of surprise and delight, which significantly enhances the reciprocity effect. This can be achieved by unexpected gestures such as sending handwritten thank-you notes, offering personalized discounts or gifts, or providing exclusive access to special events or promotions. These acts of generosity can leave a lasting impression on customers and strengthen their loyalty to the business.

3. BUILD RELATIONSHIPS

Reciprocity thrives in relationships built on trust and genuine connections. Investing time and effort in building strong relationships with customers, partners, and stakeholders can create a sense of goodwill and reciprocity. This can be achieved through regular communication, seeking feedback and input, and demonstrating authentic care for their needs and concerns. By fostering strong relationships, businesses can unlock the reciprocal benefits of trust, loyalty, and support.

4. COLLABORATE AND GIVE BACK

Reciprocity extends beyond the realm of customer relationships. Businesses can also apply this rule in their collaborations with other organizations or communities. By actively seeking opportunities to collaborate, share resources, and support worthy causes, businesses can create a network of reciprocity. This can result in mutual benefits, increased visibility, and a positive reputation within the industry.

5. CUSTOMIZE OFFERS AND INCENTIVES

Tailoring offers and incentives to individual customers can amplify the reciprocity effect. Personalized discounts, rewards programs, or exclusive perks based on customers' preferences, purchase history, or engagement can make them feel acknowledged and appreciated. This personalized approach enhances the reciprocity response and encourages customers to continue their relationship with the business. In conclusion, the Rule of Reciprocity is a powerful tool that businesses can utilize to foster strong relationships, enhance customer loyalty, and create mutually beneficial partnerships. By providing value, surprising and delighting customers, building relationships, collaborating, and customizing offers, businesses can tap into the inherent human desire to reciprocate. As a result, they can create a positive feedback loop of goodwill, trust, and success in the competitive business landscape.

Chapter 7: The Law of Cause and Effect

The Law of Cause and Effect is a fundamental principle that states that every action has a corresponding consequence. In other words, every effect can be traced back to a specific cause or series of causes. This principle applies not only to the physical world but also to the business environment. Understanding the Law of Cause and Effect is crucial for business owners as it allows them to make informed decisions, predict outcomes, and take appropriate actions. By recognizing the cause and effect relationship, businesses can identify the factors that lead to success or failure and adjust their strategies accordingly. One of the key aspects of the Law of Cause and Effect is the concept of causation. Causation refers to the direct relationship between a cause and its effect. It implies that changes in one variable will directly impact another variable. For example, if a business increases its marketing efforts, it can expect to see an increase in customer awareness and potentially higher sales. By understanding the Law of Cause and Effect, business owners can:

1. ANALYZE PAST PERFORMANCE:

By analyzing past performance, businesses can identify the causes of their successes and failures. This analysis allows them to determine which strategies and actions contributed to positive outcomes and which ones had negative consequences. Armed with this knowledge, business owners can replicate successful strategies and avoid repeating costly mistakes.

2. MAKE INFORMED DECISIONS:

When faced with critical decisions, business owners can use the Law of Cause and Effect to evaluate potential outcomes. By carefully considering the factors that contribute to success or failure, they can make more informed decisions that align with their goals and objectives. This principle helps them anticipate the consequences of their actions and choose the best course of action.

3. IMPLEMENT EFFECTIVE SOLUTIONS:

When encountering challenges or problems in their business operations, understanding the Law of Cause and Effect can aid business owners in finding effective solutions. By identifying the root causes of these challenges, they can implement targeted strategies to address the underlying issues and improve overall performance. This approach allows for more efficient problem-solving and reduces the likelihood of recurring issues.

4. PLAN TOWARDS DESIRED OUTCOMES:

By understanding the cause and effect relationship, business owners can develop proactive strategies that lead to desired outcomes. They can identify the key factors that contribute to success and focus their efforts on optimizing those aspects of their business. This approach helps in setting clear goals, allocating resources effectively, and developing comprehensive action plans. In conclusion, the Law of Cause and Effect is a powerful principle that individuals and businesses can leverage to achieve desired results. By recognizing that every action has consequences, business owners can make informed decisions, analyze past performance, implement effective solutions, and plan towards their desired outcomes. Embracing the Law of Cause and Effect can lead to improved business performance, enhanced problem-solving abilities, and increased overall success.

Chapter 8: The Rule of Consistency

Consistency is a key principle that can greatly impact the success of a business. The Rule of Consistency states that people have a strong desire to behave consistently with their previous actions, beliefs, or commitments. This principle can be applied in various aspects of business operations, from customer interactions to internal processes. One application of the Rule of Consistency is in building brand loyalty. When customers have a positive experience with a product or service, they are more likely to become repeat customers. By consistently delivering high-quality products and exceptional customer service, businesses can build a strong reputation and loyal customer base. Consistency is also important in marketing and communication efforts. When businesses consistently convey their brand message and values through various channels, including advertising, social media, and content marketing, they establish a coherent and compelling brand identity. This consistency creates a sense of trust and familiarity among consumers, making them more likely to engage with and purchase from the business. Internally, the Rule of Consistency can help streamline processes and improve efficiency. By establishing clear and consistent procedures and protocols, businesses can reduce errors and minimize the need for rework. Consistency in decision-making and leadership practices also fosters a sense of stability and trust among employees, leading to higher job satisfaction and productivity. To effectively apply the Rule of Consistency in business, here are some key strategies: 1. Clearly define and communicate your brand values and mission: Ensure that your team understands and embraces these values, and consistently integrate them into all aspects of your business operations. 2. Develop standardized processes and workflows: Establish consistent procedures for tasks and operations to ensure efficiency and minimize errors. Document these processes and provide training to employees. 3. Monitor and enforce consistency: Regularly review and assess the implementation of consistent practices across all areas of your business. Provide feedback and support to employees to ensure adherence to standards. 4. Be reliable and deliver on promises: Consistently meet customer expectations by delivering products or services on time and as promised. This builds trust and reinforces loyalty. 5. Continuously improve and adapt: While consistency is important, it's also essential to adapt to changing market trends and customer needs. Regularly evaluate your processes and strategies to identify areas for improvement and make necessary adjustments. In conclusion, the Rule of Consistency emphasizes the importance of maintaining consistency in business operations, brand messaging, and customer experiences. By consistently delivering on promises, communicating a clear brand identity, and establishing standardized processes, businesses can build trust with customers, enhance internal efficiency, and ultimately achieve long-term success.

Chapter 9: The Law of Scarcity

The Law of Scarcity is a fundamental principle in economics and business that states that limited resources are insufficient to satisfy unlimited wants and needs. In other words, there is never enough of everything to fulfill everyone's desires. As a result, scarcity creates a valuable and desirable condition. Scarcity is pervasive in the business world, impacting various aspects such as supply, demand, pricing, decision-making, and consumer behavior. Understanding and leveraging the Law of Scarcity can lead to significant advantages for businesses. One way businesses can utilize the Law of Scarcity is through product scarcity. By intentionally limiting the availability of a product or service, businesses can create a sense of exclusivity and desirability among consumers. This scarcity can be achieved by producing a limited quantity of the product or having limited-time offers and promotions. This strategy often generates increased demand as customers perceive the product as more valuable due to its rarity. Limited-edition products or special releases are examples of using scarcity as a marketing strategy. Brands like Apple and Supreme have successfully employed this tactic, creating a sense of urgency and desirability around their products. Customers line up outside stores and eagerly await product releases, knowing that if they do not act quickly, they may miss out. Scarcity can also be utilized in service-based industries. For example, some restaurants only accept a limited number of reservations each night, creating a sense of exclusivity and high demand. This scarcity drives customers to make reservations well in advance, ensuring full occupancy and reducing the risk of no-shows. Furthermore, scarcity can be applied to pricing strategies.

Businesses can create a perception of scarcity by offering limited-time discounts or price reductions. Customers are more likely to make a purchase if they believe they are getting a deal that may not be available in the future. However, it is essential for businesses to strike a balance when using the Law of Scarcity. Too much scarcity can potentially backfire and create negative perceptions among consumers. Customers may become frustrated or feel manipulated if scarcity tactics are overused or misrepresent the actual availability of a product or service. To effectively apply the Law of Scarcity, businesses should: 1. Understand their target market: Different customer segments have varying degrees of sensitivity to scarcity. Tailor scarcity tactics based on customer preferences and behaviors. 2. Create genuine scarcity: Ensure that scarcity is based on real limitations rather than artificial ones. Misleading customers about scarcity can damage trust and reputation. 3. Communicate effectively: Clearly communicate the limited availability of a product or time-limited offer to create a sense of urgency and encourage customers to take action. 4. Monitor and adjust: Continuously monitor the effectiveness of scarcity strategies and make adjustments based on customer feedback and market dynamics. In conclusion, the Law of Scarcity is a powerful tool that businesses can utilize to create desirability and drive customer actions. By understanding customer behavior, properly communicating scarcity, and offering genuine limited opportunities, businesses can leverage scarcity to increase demand, create brand loyalty, and ultimately achieve business success.

Chapter 10: The Rule of Social Proof

Social Proof is a powerful psychological principle that influences our decision-making process. It is based on the idea that people tend to look to others for guidance in uncertain situations, assuming that the actions or choices of others reflect the correct behavior. In the context of business, the Rule of Social Proof states that people are more likely to trust and follow the actions and recommendations of others if they perceive them as similar to themselves. Social proof can be applied in various aspects of business to build credibility, gain trust, and influence customer behavior. Here are some key strategies for leveraging the Rule of Social Proof:

1. CUSTOMER TESTIMONIALS AND REVIEWS

Displaying customer testimonials and reviews on your website or other marketing materials can significantly impact potential customers' perception of your products or services. Positive reviews and testimonials from satisfied customers act as social proof, demonstrating that others have had a positive experience with your brand. Encourage satisfied customers to leave reviews or provide testimonials, and showcase them prominently to build trust with potential customers.

2. INFLUENCER ENDORSEMENTS

Influencer marketing has become a popular strategy for leveraging social proof. Collaborating with influencers who align with your brand values and target audience can help you reach a wider customer base. When influencers endorse your products or services, their followers are more likely to trust and consider purchasing from your brand. However, it is essential to choose influencers who genuinely appreciate your offerings and have an authentic connection with your brand.

3. CASE STUDIES AND SUCCESS STORIES

Sharing case studies and success stories of how your products or services have helped customers achieve their goals or solve their problems can be a powerful form of social proof. Potential customers are more likely to trust your brand if they see real-world examples of how your offerings have delivered value to others. Highlight the challenges your customers faced, the solutions you provided, and the measurable results they achieved.

4. SOCIAL MEDIA ENGAGEMENT AND FOLLOWERS

Having a significant following on social media platforms can act as social proof, signaling to potential customers that your brand is popular and trusted by others. Focus on building an engaged and loyal social media community by consistently sharing valuable content, responding to comments and messages, and actively engaging with your followers. Encourage your existing customers to follow and engage with you on social media, amplifying your social proof.

5. INDUSTRY AWARDS AND RECOGNITIONS

Publicize any industry awards, certifications, or recognitions your business has received. These external validations serve as social proof, signaling to potential customers that your brand is reputable and trustworthy. Display these achievements on your website, marketing materials, and social media platforms.

6. TRUST SEALS AND CERTIFICATIONS

Trust seals and certifications, such as SSL certificates, privacy certifications, or security badges, provide reassurance to customers that their sensitive information is protected when interacting with your brand. Display these trust seals prominently on your website, especially during the checkout process, to alleviate any concerns potential customers may have about sharing their personal information.

7. USER-GENERATED CONTENT

Encourage your customers to create and share user-generated content related to your brand, products, or services. This can include customer photos, videos, or testimonials. By showcasing user-generated content on your website and social media platforms, you provide social proof that others are actively engaged with your brand and finding value in your offerings.

8. PARTNERING WITH ESTABLISHED BRANDS OR INFLUENCERS

Partnering with established brands or influencers in your industry can significantly enhance your social proof.

Collaborations with well-known brands or influencers reflect positively on the credibility and quality of your offerings. Seek out partnerships that align with your brand values and target audience to leverage their reputation and influence. In conclusion, the Rule of Social Proof is a powerful tool in building credibility, gaining trust, and influencing customer behavior. By strategically implementing social proof strategies such as customer testimonials, influencer endorsements, case studies, social media engagement, industry awards, trust seals, user-generated content, and partnerships, businesses can effectively leverage the psychological principle of social proof to attract and convert potential customers.

Chapter 11: The Law of Competition

In the world of business, competition is inevitable. Whether you are operating in a local market or on a global scale, understanding and leveraging the Law of Competition is essential for success. This chapter will explore the key principles of competition and how businesses can navigate this dynamic landscape to thrive.

THE NATURE OF COMPETITION

Competition is the driving force behind innovation, growth, and progress in the business world. It involves competing with other businesses in a given market to gain an advantage and attract customers. Here are some key aspects of the Law of Competition:

1. Multiple Players

Competition implies the presence of multiple players, each vying for a share of the market. These players can be direct competitors offering similar products or services, or they can be indirect competitors offering substitute options. Understanding the competitive landscape is crucial for identifying opportunities and positioning your business effectively.

2. Customer-Centric Approach

In a competitive market, customers hold the power to choose between different businesses. This highlights the importance of adopting a customer-centric approach. By understanding and addressing the needs and preferences of your target audience, you can gain a competitive edge and attract loyal customers.

3. Differentiation

To stand out in a competitive market, businesses need to differentiate themselves from their competitors. This can be done through various means, such as offering unique features, superior quality, exceptional customer service, or innovative solutions. Finding your unique selling proposition and effectively communicating it to your target audience is key.

4. Continuous Improvement

Competition is not static; it is an ongoing process. Businesses must strive for continuous improvement in order to stay ahead. This can involve investing in research and development, staying up-to-date with industry trends, and continuously refining products, services, and processes.

STRATEGIES FOR COMPETING EFFECTIVELY

Competing effectively requires a strategic approach. Here are some strategies to help businesses navigate the Law of Competition:

1. Market Research

Thorough market research is essential for understanding your target audience, identifying competitors, and uncovering untapped market opportunities. By gathering data and insights, you can make informed decisions and develop strategies that align with market demands.

2. Differentiation and Unique Value Proposition

Differentiation is crucial to gain a competitive edge. Identify what sets your business apart from competitors and develop a unique value proposition. This could be through product features, pricing, customer service, branding, or other factors. Clearly communicate this unique value proposition to your target audience.

3. Focus on Customer Experience

One of the most effective ways to stand out in a competitive market is by providing exceptional customer experiences. Focus on building relationships with your customers, understanding their needs, and delivering outstanding service at every touchpoint. By exceeding customer expectations, you can foster loyalty and gain a competitive advantage.

4. Continuous Innovation

Innovation is key to staying competitive. Keep an eye on industry trends, listen to customer feedback, and invest in research and development. Continuously seek ways to improve your products, services, and processes to meet the evolving needs of your customers and stay ahead of the competition.

5. Collaborate and Build Strategic Partnerships

Collaborating with other businesses can be mutually beneficial and help you expand your reach. Look for opportunities to form strategic partnerships that can enhance your offerings, reach new markets, or improve operational efficiency. Combining resources and expertise can give you a competitive advantage.

6. Monitor and Adapt

Competition is dynamic, so it's important to continuously monitor your competitors, market trends, and customer preferences. Be prepared to adapt your strategies and offerings to stay relevant and competitive. Embrace a mindset of agility and flexibility in order to quickly respond to changes in the market.

CONCLUSION

The Law of Competition shapes the business landscape and provides both challenges and opportunities. By understanding the nature of competition and implementing effective strategies, businesses can not only survive but thrive in a competitive market. Remember to differentiate, focus on the customer, continuously innovate, collaborate, and adapt to stay ahead of the competition and achieve long-term success.

Chapter 12: The Rule of Innovation

In today's fast-paced and competitive business environment, the Rule of Innovation plays a critical role in driving growth, gaining a competitive edge, and ensuring long-term success. The ability to innovate is essential for businesses to adapt to changing market trends, customer preferences, and technological advancements.

THE POWER OF INNOVATION

Innovation is not limited to the development of groundbreaking products or services. It encompasses a wide range of activities, including process improvements, business model innovation, and creating a culture of innovation within the organization. It requires a mindset that embraces change, encourages creativity, and fosters continuous improvement. Effective innovation allows businesses to: 1. Stay Ahead of the Competition: Innovation enables businesses to differentiate themselves from competitors by offering unique and valuable solutions to customer problems. By continuously improving and introducing new ideas, products, or services, companies can maintain their relevance and attract and retain customers. 2. Enhance Customer Experience: Innovations that focus on improving the customer experience can significantly impact customer satisfaction and loyalty. By understanding customer needs and pain points, businesses can develop innovative solutions that exceed expectations and create a memorable experience. 3. Increase Efficiency and Productivity: Innovation can streamline internal processes, automate tasks, and eliminate bottlenecks, leading to improved efficiency and productivity. By embracing new technologies and systems, businesses can optimize their operations and achieve cost savings. 4. Identify New Market Opportunities: Innovation allows businesses to identify and seize new market opportunities. By conducting market research, identifying emerging trends, and listening to customer feedback, companies can uncover untapped markets or develop innovative solutions for existing ones. 5. Foster a Culture of Creativity and Learning: Building a culture that encourages and rewards innovation can unleash the creative potential of employees. Businesses that cultivate an environment of curiosity, experimentation, and collaboration often experience higher levels of employee engagement and satisfaction, leading to better ideas and outcomes.

STRATEGIES FOR FOSTERING INNOVATION

To embrace the Rule of Innovation and drive meaningful change within their organizations, business owners can implement the following strategies: 1. Encourage Idea Generation: Foster a culture where everyone feels empowered to contribute ideas. Establish platforms for employees to share their suggestions, such as idea incubators, suggestion boxes, or brainstorming sessions. 2. Invest in Research and Development: Allocate resources to research and development initiatives focused on understanding market trends, emerging technologies, and customer preferences. This investment can lead to the development of innovative products, services, or processes. 3. Embrace Risk-Taking: Encourage calculated risks and provide a safe space for employees to experiment and learn from failures. Create a culture that views failures as valuable learning opportunities rather than setbacks. 4. Collaborate and Seek External Insights: Foster collaborations with external partners, including customers, suppliers, universities, and industry experts. These partnerships can bring fresh perspectives, knowledge, and resources that can fuel innovation efforts. 5. Provide Training and Development: Invest in ongoing training and development programs to enhance employees' skills and stimulate their creative and problem-solving abilities. Offer workshops, seminars, or online courses to foster a mindset of continuous learning. 6. Establish an Innovation Team: Create a dedicated team responsible for driving innovation within the organization. This team can be tasked with researching market trends, exploring new technologies, and developing innovation initiatives.

MEASURING THE IMPACT OF INNOVATION

Measuring the impact of innovation is crucial to understand the effectiveness of your efforts and guide future innovation strategies. Key performance indicators (KPIs) to consider include: 1. Revenue from New Products or Services: Measure the financial contribution of new offerings to assess their success in generating revenue. 2. Customer Satisfaction and Loyalty: Track customer feedback, surveys, and retention rates to gauge the impact of innovation on customer satisfaction and loyalty. 3. Employee Engagement and Satisfaction: Monitor employee engagement levels and satisfaction surveys to measure the impact of your innovation initiatives on your workforce. 4. Efficiency and Productivity: Assess improvements in process efficiency, productivity, and cost savings resulting from innovation initiatives. 5. Market Share and Competitive Advantage: Monitor changes in market share and assess your competitive position through market research and analysis. By regularly evaluating these KPIs, businesses can gauge the effectiveness of their innovation efforts, identify areas for improvement, and make data-driven decisions to drive future innovation.

INNOVATION FOR SUCCESS

Embracing the Rule of Innovation is vital for businesses looking to thrive in today's dynamic and competitive landscape. It is not just about developing groundbreaking products or services but also about fostering a culture of creativity, continuous learning, and improvement. By prioritizing innovation and investing in research and development, businesses can stay relevant, meet evolving customer needs, and achieve sustainable growth.

Chapter 13: The Law of Trust

Trust is a fundamental principle in any business relationship. It plays a vital role in establishing credibility, fostering strong customer relationships, and ensuring long-term success. The Law of Trust states that trust is the foundation of any successful business interaction and that it must be earned and maintained. Building trust starts with consistent and reliable actions. When customers can rely on a business to deliver on its promises, it fosters a sense of trust and confidence in the brand. Trust is built over time through positive experiences, open communication, and transparency. One key aspect of building trust is delivering high-quality products or services. Consistently providing value and exceeding customer expectations helps establish trust and loyalty. When customers can depend on a business to consistently meet their needs and deliver superior products, they are more likely to trust the brand and continue their patronage. Another important factor in building trust is effective communication. Open and transparent communication helps establish a strong relationship between a business and its customers. Clear and honest communication builds credibility and reliability, which are essential elements of trust. Trust also extends to the relationships between businesses and their employees. A supportive and trusting work environment fosters employee loyalty, engagement, and productivity. When employees trust their leaders and feel trusted in return, they are more likely to go above and beyond to contribute to the success of the business. To build and maintain trust, businesses should prioritize the following strategies:

1. BE TRANSPARENT

Transparency is key in establishing trust. Communicate openly and honestly with customers and employees about policies, pricing, and any changes that may affect them. Transparent communication builds credibility and fosters an environment of trust.

2. DELIVER ON PROMISES

Consistently deliver on your promises and commitments. When customers have confidence that you will fulfill their expectations, it builds trust in your brand. This includes delivering products and services on time, as described, and to the expected quality standards.

3. PROVIDE EXCELLENT CUSTOMER SERVICE

Offering exceptional customer service is crucial in building trust. Respond promptly to customer inquiries and concerns, and go above and beyond to resolve any issues. Providing a positive customer experience builds trust and encourages customer loyalty.

4. MAINTAIN CONFIDENTIALITY

Respect customer and employee confidentiality. Protect sensitive information and ensure that it is not shared or used inappropriately. Demonstrating respect for privacy builds trust and shows your commitment to ethical practices.

5. BUILD STRONG RELATIONSHIPS

Invest in building strong relationships with customers, employees, suppliers, and other stakeholders. Develop meaningful connections based on trust, mutual respect, and shared values. Building strong relationships fosters trust and contributes to long-term success.

6. CONTINUOUSLY IMPROVE

Strive for continuous improvement in all aspects of your business. Regularly seek feedback from customers and employees, and use their input to make necessary changes and enhancements. Demonstrating a commitment to growth and improvement instills trust in your ability to adapt and meet evolving needs. Trust is a valuable and delicate asset for any business. It takes time and consistent effort to build, but once established, it can lead to customer loyalty, positive word-of-mouth, and long-term success. By prioritizing transparency, delivering on promises, providing excellent customer service, maintaining confidentiality, building strong relationships, and continuously striving for improvement, businesses can cultivate trust and create a foundation for sustainable growth.

Chapter 14: The Rule of Decision Making

When it comes to running a business, decision making is an essential skill that can greatly impact its success or failure. The Rule of Decision Making emphasizes the importance of making informed and strategic decisions for long-term growth and sustainability. In this chapter, we will explore the key principles and strategies to optimize the decision-making process in a business context.

UNDERSTANDING THE RULE OF DECISION MAKING

The Rule of Decision Making states that effective decision making is based on a systematic and rational approach. It involves gathering relevant information, analyzing potential outcomes, considering the risks and benefits, and ultimately choosing the best course of action. By following this rule, business owners and leaders can minimize the potential for errors, improve problem-solving abilities, and enhance overall business performance.

Key Principles of Effective Decision Making

1. **Define clear objectives:** Before making any decision, it is crucial to define the goals and objectives that the decision aims to achieve. This clarity ensures that the decision aligns with the broader strategic vision of the business. 2. **Gather relevant information:** Making informed decisions requires gathering reliable and accurate information. This may involve conducting market research, analyzing financial data, consulting experts, or seeking feedback from stakeholders. 3. **Analyze potential outcomes:** Consider the potential consequences of each decision option. This involves evaluating the risks, benefits, costs, and potential impact on various aspects of the business, such as finances, operations, employees, and customers. 4. **Weigh pros and cons:** Conduct a thorough analysis of the advantages and disadvantages of each decision option. This helps in assessing the trade-offs and

determining the best course of action. 5. **Consider long-term implications:** Effective decision making requires considering the long-term implications and sustainability of the chosen option. Avoid making decisions solely based on short-term gains or immediate needs. 6. **Involve key stakeholders:** Consult and involve relevant stakeholders in the decision-making process. This can include employees, customers, suppliers, and investors. Their input can provide valuable insights and help in making more inclusive and well-rounded decisions. 7. **Manage risks:** Assess and manage the potential risks associated with the decision. This may involve developing contingency plans, allocating resources for risk mitigation, or seeking expert advice to minimize the negative impact of potential risks.

Strategies for Effective Decision Making

1. **Utilize data-driven analysis:** Make decisions based on data and factual information rather than relying solely on intuition or subjective opinions. This approach ensures objectivity and minimizes biases. 2. **Incorporate diverse perspectives:** Encourage diverse viewpoints and opinions in the decision-making process. This diversity brings in different insights and creative solutions, leading to more comprehensive decision outcomes. 3. **Consider alternative options:** Explore multiple decision options before settling on a final choice. This allows for a more thorough evaluation of various possibilities and increases the likelihood of making the best decision. 4. **Implement a decision-making framework:** Establish a structured decision-making framework tailored to the business's needs. This framework should outline the steps,

responsibilities, and criteria for decision making to ensure consistency and efficiency. 5. **Evaluate and learn from past decisions:** Assess the outcomes of previous decisions to identify areas for improvement. This analysis helps in refining the decision-making process and avoiding repeating past mistakes. 6. **Balance intuition and analysis:** While data and analysis are vital, don't overlook intuitive judgment. Sometimes, relying on gut instincts or intuition can provide valuable insights and guide decision making, especially in uncertain situations. 7. **Communicate decisions effectively:** Once a decision is made, communicate it clearly to all relevant stakeholders. Ensuring effective communication helps in gaining buy-in, minimizing confusion, and facilitating the smooth implementation of decisions. By following the Rule of Decision Making and applying these strategies, businesses can foster a culture of effective decision making, resulting in improved outcomes, increased efficiency, and a competitive edge in the market.

Conclusion

Effective decision making is a crucial skill for business owners and leaders. By understanding and applying the Rule of Decision Making, businesses can enhance their problem-solving abilities, minimize risks, and make informed choices that contribute to long-term success. By incorporating the key principles and strategies discussed in this chapter, business owners can optimize their decision-making process and drive sustainable growth.

Chapter 15: The Law of Integrity

Integrity is a fundamental principle for achieving long-term success and building a reputable business. It is the adherence to moral and ethical principles, honesty, and consistency in actions and values. The Law of Integrity states that businesses that operate with integrity establish trust with customers, employees, partners, and other stakeholders, leading to sustainable growth and a positive reputation.

THE IMPORTANCE OF INTEGRITY IN BUSINESS

Integrity is crucial in business for several reasons. Here are some key reasons why the law of integrity is essential:

1. Establishing Trust

Integrity builds trust, which is the foundation of any successful business relationship. When customers, employees, and partners perceive a business as trustworthy, they are more likely to engage, collaborate, and remain loyal. Trust also helps businesses navigate challenges and conflicts more effectively.

2. Enhancing Reputation

A strong reputation is invaluable in today's competitive business landscape. Businesses with a reputation for integrity attract more customers, top talent, and strategic partnerships. A positive reputation serves as a differentiator, setting a business apart from competitors and creating a sense of credibility and reliability.

3. Fostering Employee Engagement

Integrity plays a significant role in creating a positive work environment. When employees witness leaders acting with integrity and upholding ethical values, they feel more engaged, motivated, and loyal. A culture of integrity inspires employees to uphold the same values, leading to a more productive and harmonious workplace.

4. Mitigating Risks

Operating with integrity helps businesses avoid legal and ethical issues that can damage their reputation and bottom line. By adhering to ethical standards and legal requirements, businesses reduce the risk of lawsuits, regulatory penalties, and negative publicity. This, in turn, protects their brand image and ensures business continuity.

5. Attracting and Retaining Customers

Customers want to do business with companies that demonstrate integrity. When businesses prioritize honesty, transparency, and ethical practices, they attract customers who value those principles. By consistently delivering on promises and providing exceptional customer service, businesses can build long-lasting relationships with their customers.

6. Promoting Collaboration and Partnerships

Partnerships and collaborations are essential for business growth. Businesses that operate with integrity are more likely to attract like-minded partners who share the same values. Trustworthy and ethical businesses are seen as reliable, making them an ideal choice for strategic alliances and joint ventures.

INTEGRATING INTEGRITY INTO BUSINESS PRACTICES

To apply the Law of Integrity effectively, businesses should incorporate ethical practices into their everyday operations. Here are some strategies for integrating integrity into business practices:

1. Define and Communicate Core Values

Develop and communicate a well-defined set of core values that emphasize integrity, honesty, and ethical behavior. These values should guide decision-making at all levels of the organization and serve as a compass for actions and behaviors.

2. Lead by Example

Leaders play a crucial role in setting the tone for integrity within an organization. They should demonstrate integrity through their actions, decisions, and interactions with stakeholders. This commitment to integrity will trickle down and influence the entire workforce.

3. Establish Clear Policies and Procedures

Develop and implement policies and procedures that reinforce integrity and ethical conduct. These guidelines should cover areas such as conflicts of interest, anti-corruption measures, data privacy, and protection of sensitive information. Regularly train employees on these policies to ensure awareness and compliance.

4. Encourage Whistleblowing

Create a culture that encourages employees to speak up about unethical or illegal activities. Establish anonymous reporting mechanisms to protect whistleblowers and provide appropriate channels for reporting potential misconduct. Address reported issues promptly and take appropriate action to maintain trust and integrity.

5. Regularly Monitor and Assess Compliance

Implement systems to monitor and assess compliance with ethical standards and legal requirements. Conduct regular audits, reviews, and assessments to identify areas of improvement and ensure adherence to ethical practices. Address any gaps or issues that arise promptly and transparently.

6. Foster Open Communication

Encourage open and transparent communication within the organization. Create channels for employees to express concerns, provide feedback, and share ideas. Nurture an environment where everyone feels comfortable speaking up about potential ethical dilemmas or conflicts of interest.

7. Continuously Improve

Strive for continuous improvement in ethical practices. Regularly review and update policies, procedures, and training programs to reflect evolving ethical standards and best practices. Seek feedback from employees, customers, and other stakeholders to identify areas for improvement and innovation.

CONCLUSION

Operating with integrity is not just about following the rules; it is about consistently acting in an ethical and honest manner. The Law of Integrity emphasizes the importance of building trust, fostering a positive reputation, and establishing a culture of integrity within an organization. By integrating integrity into business practices, businesses can create a strong foundation for long-term success, growth, and positive stakeholder relationships.

Chapter 16: The Rule of Time Management

Effective time management is crucial for business owners to maximize productivity, achieve goals, and create a healthy work-life balance. The Rule of Time Management emphasizes the importance of prioritizing tasks and utilizing time efficiently to optimize performance and achieve success.

THE VALUE OF TIME

Time is a valuable and limited resource that cannot be replenished or recovered once it is gone. It is essential for business owners to recognize the value of their time and make conscious efforts to manage it effectively. By understanding the Rule of Time Management, business owners can make informed decisions about how they allocate their time and prioritize their tasks.

SETTING CLEAR GOALS

The first step in effective time management is setting clear and specific goals. By establishing goals, business owners can prioritize their tasks and focus their efforts on activities that align with their objectives. Setting SMART (Specific, Measurable, Achievable, Relevant, and Time-bound) goals can provide a clear framework for organizing and managing time.

IDENTIFYING PRIORITIES

Once goals are established, it is important to identify priorities. The Rule of Time Management suggests that not all tasks or activities hold the same level of importance or urgency. Business owners should assess their tasks and categorize them based on their significance and impact on their goals. This will help them allocate their time accordingly and focus on high-priority tasks that contribute directly to their objectives.

PRIORITIZATION TECHNIQUES

There are various techniques that business owners can use to prioritize their tasks effectively: 1. Eisenhower Matrix: This matrix categorizes tasks into four quadrants based on their urgency and importance. It helps business owners identify and prioritize tasks that are both urgent and important, while delegating or eliminating tasks that are not. 2. Pareto Analysis: Also known as the 80/20 rule, this technique suggests that 80% of results come from 20% of efforts. By identifying the most critical tasks that contribute the most to desired outcomes, business owners can focus their time and efforts on activities that yield the greatest impact. 3. Time Blocking: This technique involves scheduling specific time blocks for different types of tasks. By assigning dedicated time slots for different activities, business owners can avoid multitasking, reduce distractions, and improve focus and productivity. 4. ABC Method: This method involves categorizing tasks into three categories: A tasks (high-priority and high-impact tasks), B tasks (medium-priority tasks), and C tasks (low-priority tasks). Business owners can then focus on completing A tasks before moving on to B and C tasks.

ELIMINATING TIME WASTERS

To effectively manage time, business owners must identify and eliminate time-wasting activities. This includes avoiding distractions such as excessive social media use, unnecessary meetings, unproductive interruptions, and procrastination. By being mindful of how time is spent and making conscious efforts to eliminate time wasters, business owners can optimize their productivity and efficiency.

DELEGATING AND OUTSOURCING

The Rule of Time Management also emphasizes the importance of delegation and outsourcing. Business owners should delegate tasks that can be done by others, allowing them to focus on high-priority activities that require their expertise. Outsourcing certain tasks to external professionals or agencies can also free up valuable time and resources, enabling business owners to concentrate on core business operations.

TIME MANAGEMENT TOOLS AND TECHNIQUES

Numerous time management tools and techniques are available to assist business owners in managing their time effectively. These tools range from digital calendars and task management apps to project management software and time tracking tools. Business owners should explore different tools and techniques to find the ones that best suit their needs and preferences.

CONTINUOUS IMPROVEMENT

Time management is an ongoing process that requires continuous improvement and adjustment. Business owners should regularly evaluate their time management strategies, assess their effectiveness, and make necessary changes to optimize their productivity and time allocation. By embracing a mindset of continuous improvement, business owners can establish efficient time management practices that support their long-term success. In conclusion, the Rule of Time Management highlights the importance of prioritizing tasks, setting clear goals, and utilizing time efficiently to optimize productivity and achieve business success. By implementing effective time management strategies, business owners can make the most of their valuable resource and create a well-balanced and successful business.

Chapter 17: The Law of Focus

In today's fast-paced and highly competitive business world, the ability to stay focused is crucial for success. The Law of Focus states that concentrating your efforts on a specific goal or task increases your chances of achieving it. In business, there are often numerous tasks, projects, and opportunities competing for our attention and resources. However, spreading ourselves too thin can lead to inefficiencies, decreased productivity, and ultimately, subpar results. By understanding and applying the Law of Focus, we can prioritize our efforts and maximize our chances of attaining our desired outcomes.

THE IMPORTANCE OF FOCUS IN BUSINESS

Focus allows us to direct our energy and resources towards the most important and impactful activities. It enables us to concentrate our efforts on tasks that align with our overall strategic objectives. Here are a few key reasons why the Law of Focus is important in business: 1. Efficiency: Focusing on specific tasks or projects allows us to streamline our operations and use our resources effectively. By concentrating on what truly matters, we can eliminate distractions and avoid wasting time, effort, and money on non-essential activities. 2. Productivity: When we focus on one task at a time, we can devote our full attention to it. This focused effort enhances our productivity and enables us to accomplish tasks more efficiently. Studies have shown that multitasking can actually decrease productivity, as it takes time for our brains to switch between tasks. 3. Quality: The Law of Focus encourages us to prioritize quality over quantity. By focusing on a smaller number of tasks or projects, we can dedicate more time and attention to each one. This leads to better quality outcomes, as we can thoroughly analyze, plan, and execute our work. 4. Decision-making: When we have a clear focus, it becomes easier to make decisions. We can assess the costs, benefits, and risks associated with each option and select the one that aligns best with our goals. Focus provides clarity and direction in decision-making, reducing the likelihood of making impulsive or ineffective choices. 5. Competitive Advantage: Businesses that focus on their core competencies and areas of expertise gain a competitive edge. By specializing and becoming known for a specific product or service, businesses can attract a niche market and differentiate themselves from competitors. Focus allows businesses to excel in their chosen areas and stand out among the competition.

STRATEGIES TO APPLY THE LAW OF FOCUS

To apply the Law of Focus effectively in your business, consider the following strategies: 1. Set Clear Goals: Clearly define your objectives and identify the key outcomes you want to achieve. Setting specific, measurable, achievable, relevant, and time-bound (SMART) goals provides a framework for your focus. 2. Prioritize Tasks: Evaluate each task or project based on its importance and impact. Prioritize your efforts accordingly, focusing on activities that align with your goals and have the highest potential for success. 3. Delegate and Outsource: Identify tasks that can be delegated to others or outsourced to external providers. By entrusting certain responsibilities to capable individuals or organizations, you can free up your time and energy to focus on critical tasks that require your expertise. 4. Avoid Multitasking: Resist the temptation to multitask, as it diminishes focus and decreases productivity. Instead, focus on one task at a time and allocate dedicated blocks of time for specific activities. This enables you to concentrate fully and complete tasks more efficiently. 5. Limit Distractions: Minimize distractions that can divert your attention and impede your focus. Create a conducive work environment by eliminating unnecessary interruptions, implementing technology tools to manage distractions, and establishing boundaries with colleagues and team members. 6. Review and Reflect: Regularly review your progress and reflect on your focus. Assess whether your efforts align with your goals and if any adjustments need to be made. Consider seeking feedback from trusted advisors or mentors to gain additional perspectives. By applying these strategies, you can harness the power of focus and significantly enhance your business performance. Embracing the Law of Focus enables you to make better decisions, achieve higher levels of efficiency and productivity, and ultimately, realize your desired outcomes.

CONCLUSION

The Law of Focus highlights the importance of concentrating our efforts on specific tasks and goals in order to achieve success in business. By avoiding multitasking, setting clear goals, prioritizing tasks, and minimizing distractions, we can harness the power of focus and increase our efficiency, productivity, and overall business performance. Remember, focus is not just about doing more; it's about doing the right things and achieving the desired results.

Chapter 18: The Rule of Leadership

Leadership plays a crucial role in the success of any business. A strong and effective leader can inspire and motivate their team to achieve their goals, drive innovation, and create a positive work environment. The Rule of Leadership emphasizes the importance of strong leadership skills and qualities in the business world.

UNDERSTANDING THE RULE OF LEADERSHIP

Effective leadership involves guiding and influencing others to achieve a common objective. It requires a combination of technical expertise, interpersonal skills, and a deep understanding of the business and industry. The Rule of Leadership states that successful leaders possess certain qualities and follow specific principles to inspire and motivate their teams.

The Qualities of a Great Leader

1. Visionary: Great leaders have a clear vision for the future and can articulate it to their team. They inspire others to work towards a shared goal and create a sense of purpose. 2. Communication skills: Effective communication is essential for leaders to convey their ideas and expectations clearly. They listen to their team members, provide feedback, and ensure everyone understands their role in achieving the vision. 3. Integrity: Leaders with integrity earn the trust and respect of their team. They act ethically and consistently, inspiring others to do the same. They lead by example and maintain transparency in their actions and decision-making. 4. Emotional intelligence: Leaders with high emotional intelligence can understand and manage their own emotions, as well as those of their team members. They are empathetic, supportive, and skilled at resolving conflicts and building strong relationships. 5. Adaptability: The business landscape is constantly evolving, and leaders

need to adapt to change. They are flexible, open to new ideas, and can navigate through uncertainty and ambiguity. 6. Decisiveness: Leaders must make tough decisions and take calculated risks. They gather the necessary information, analyze different options, and confidently make choices that align with the overall vision and goals. 7. Empowerment: Great leaders empower their teams by delegating responsibilities, encouraging creativity, and fostering a culture of innovation. They trust their employees, provide them with the necessary resources, and offer guidance and support when needed.

Principles of Effective Leadership

1. Lead by example: Leaders should embody the values and behaviors they expect from their team. By modeling the desired qualities, they inspire others to follow suit. 2. Build strong relationships: Effective leaders prioritize building relationships based on trust and respect. They invest time in getting to know their team members, understanding their strengths and weaknesses, and providing support and guidance. 3. Foster open communication: Leaders encourage open and honest communication within the team. They create a safe and supportive environment where everyone feels comfortable sharing their ideas, concerns, and feedback. 4. Develop and empower others: Great leaders invest in the development of their team members. They provide opportunities for growth, offer constructive feedback, and empower employees to take on new challenges and responsibilities. 5. Embrace diversity and inclusion: Effective leaders value diversity and create an inclusive workplace where

everyone feels valued and respected. They understand that diverse perspectives lead to stronger decision-making and innovation. 6. Continuously learn and adapt: Leadership is a lifelong journey of growth and learning. Effective leaders seek out opportunities for self-improvement, stay updated on industry trends, and adapt their leadership style based on the needs of the team and the business.

CONCLUSION

The Rule of Leadership emphasizes the importance of strong leadership in driving business success. Leadership qualities such as vision, effective communication, integrity, adaptability, and empowerment are essential for inspiring and motivating teams, fostering innovation, and creating a positive work culture. By understanding and applying these principles, business owners can become effective leaders who can navigate challenges, inspire their teams, and achieve long-term success.

Chapter 19: The Law of Teamwork

Effective teamwork is crucial for the success of any business. The Law of Teamwork emphasizes the importance of collaboration, communication, and synergy among team members. A well-functioning team can achieve greater results than individuals working independently. Here, we will explore the key principles and strategies to maximize the potential of teamwork in your business.

THE POWER OF COLLABORATION

Collaboration is the cornerstone of effective teamwork. When team members work together towards a common goal, they can combine their skills, knowledge, and experiences to achieve better outcomes. Here are some strategies to foster collaboration within your team: 1. Clear Communication: Encourage open and honest communication among team members. Create a safe and respectful environment where everyone feels comfortable expressing their ideas, concerns, and feedback. 2. Shared Vision and Goals: Ensure that all team members are aligned with the team's mission, vision, and objectives. Clearly communicate the desired outcomes and milestones to keep everyone focused and motivated. 3. Defined Roles and Responsibilities: Clarify each team member's role and responsibilities within the team. This helps avoid confusion, duplication of efforts, and conflict. Assign tasks based on individual strengths and expertise. 4. Trust and Respect: Build a culture of trust and respect within the team. Encourage collaboration rather than competition. Recognize and value each team member's contributions and abilities. 5. Collaboration Tools and Technology: Utilize collaboration tools and technology to facilitate communication, document sharing, and project management. This enhances efficiency and coordination among team members, especially in remote work environments.

EMBRACING DIVERSITY

Diversity within a team brings together different perspectives, skills, and ideas. Embracing diversity can lead to innovative solutions, improved problem-solving, and a more inclusive work environment. Here are some strategies to promote diversity within your team: 1. Inclusive Hiring Practices: Promote diversity during the hiring process by considering candidates from different backgrounds, experiences, and skill sets. Avoid unconscious bias and ensure equal opportunities for all. 2. Team Building Activities: Encourage team members to get to know each other on a personal level. Organize team-building activities that foster inclusivity, such as diversity training, cultural celebrations, or mentoring programs. 3. Active Listening: Create a culture of active listening, where team members genuinely consider and value diverse viewpoints. This fosters respect and encourages open dialogue that leads to better decision-making. 4. Conflict Resolution: Foster a healthy approach to addressing conflict within the team. Encourage open discussions and mediate conflicts by focusing on understanding and finding common ground.

EFFECTIVE LEADERSHIP

Effective leadership is crucial for guiding and supporting the team towards success. A strong leader sets the tone, motivates team members, and creates a positive work culture. Here are some key qualities and strategies for effective leadership within a team: 1. Clear Direction:

Clearly communicate goals, expectations, and deadlines. Provide guidance and support to ensure that all team members understand their roles and how their contributions fit into the bigger picture. 2. Empowerment: Encourage autonomy and empower team members to make decisions and take ownership of their work. This fosters creativity, innovation, and personal growth. 3. Recognition and Reward: Acknowledge and appreciate the efforts and achievements of individual team members and the team as a whole. This boosts morale, motivation, and a sense of belonging. 4. Continuous Learning and Development: Foster a culture of continuous learning and development within the team. Provide opportunities for skill-building, training, and professional growth. 5. Conflict Resolution: Address conflicts promptly and effectively. Act as a mediator and facilitator, promoting open communication, understanding, and compromise among team members. By harnessing the power of collaboration, embracing diversity, and practicing effective leadership, you can unlock the true potential of teamwork within your business. When team members work together towards a shared vision, utilizing their unique strengths and perspectives, extraordinary results can be achieved.

Chapter 20: The Rule of Communication

Good communication is crucial for the success of any business. It is the foundation that allows information to flow internally and externally, enabling effective collaboration, understanding, and decision-making. The Rule of Communication emphasizes the importance of clear and concise communication in all aspects of business operations.

THE POWER OF EFFECTIVE COMMUNICATION

Effective communication is a powerful tool that can bring numerous benefits to a business. It ensures that messages are delivered accurately, reduces misunderstandings, strengthens relationships, boosts productivity, improves customer satisfaction, and enhances the overall reputation of the business. Furthermore, effective communication is essential in building a positive and engaged workplace culture. It fosters transparency, trust, and collaboration among team members, allowing for better problem-solving, decision-making, and innovation.

ELEMENTS OF EFFECTIVE COMMUNICATION

To implement the Rule of Communication successfully, it is important to understand the key elements of effective communication. These include:

Clarity and Conciseness:

Messages should be clear, straightforward, and easy to understand. Avoid jargon or complex language that may confuse the recipient. Be concise and get to the point, ensuring that the message is not diluted by unnecessary details.

Active Listening:

Active listening involves fully focusing on the speaker, seeking to understand their perspective, and providing feedback or validation when necessary. It shows respect and helps in building meaningful connections with others.

Nonverbal Communication:

Nonverbal cues, such as facial expressions, body language, and tone of voice, are an important aspect of communication. They can convey emotions, intentions, and attitudes, complementing and sometimes even overriding verbal messages. Paying attention to nonverbal cues can greatly enhance communication effectiveness.

Empathy and Emotional Intelligence:

Showing empathy and emotional intelligence in communication helps create a supportive and understanding environment. Being able to recognize and respond to the emotions of others builds rapport and fosters stronger relationships.

Two-Way Communication:

Communication should not be a one-way street. Encourage open dialogue, active participation, and feedback from all parties involved. This ensures that the message is not only conveyed but also fully understood and acknowledged.

STRATEGIES FOR EFFECTIVE COMMUNICATION

Applying the Rule of Communication requires the implementation of effective communication strategies. Here are some key strategies to consider:

Establishing Clear Channels:

Create clear channels of communication within the organization, including regular team meetings, email updates, and an open-door policy. Ensure that employees are aware of these channels and feel comfortable using them to address concerns or share ideas.

Using Various Communication Methods:

Different individuals have different preferences when it comes to communication. Some may prefer face-to-face interactions, while others may be more comfortable with written communication. Utilize a range of communication methods, such as meetings, emails, phone calls, and instant messaging, to accommodate different communication styles.

Adapting Communication for Different Audiences:

Tailor your communication style and message to suit the specific needs and preferences of your audience. Consider factors such as their level of expertise, cultural background, and preferred communication methods. This helps to ensure that the message is received and understood effectively.

Providing Context and Purpose:

When communicating information or instructions, provide the necessary context and explain the purpose behind the message. This helps the recipient understand the importance and relevance of the information, increasing their engagement and motivation to act upon it.

Regularly Seeking Feedback:

Encourage open feedback from team members, customers, and other stakeholders to improve communication effectiveness. Actively listen to their suggestions and concerns, and make necessary adjustments to enhance future communication processes.

CONCLUSION

The Rule of Communication highlights the significance of effective communication in all aspects of business. By implementing strategies that promote clear and concise communication, businesses can enhance productivity, improve relationships, and achieve their goals more efficiently. Remember, communication is a skill that can always be refined and improved, and by prioritizing it, business owners can set their organizations on a path to long-term success.

Chapter 21: The Law of Negotiation

Negotiation is a fundamental skill in business that involves reaching mutually beneficial agreements between parties. The Law of Negotiation states that successful negotiations require effective communication, strategic thinking, and the ability to find common ground.

UNDERSTANDING THE LAW OF NEGOTIATION

Negotiation is a process where two or more parties discuss and propose solutions to reach a mutually satisfactory agreement. It plays a crucial role in various aspects of business, including contracts, partnerships, sales, and resolving conflicts. The Law of Negotiation is based on the principles of fairness, collaboration, and finding win-win solutions. It requires active listening, empathy, and understanding the needs and interests of all parties involved. Successful negotiators focus on creating value and maintaining relationships, rather than pursuing a strictly competitive approach.

KEY STRATEGIES FOR SUCCESSFUL NEGOTIATION

1. Preparation: Thoroughly prepare for negotiations by researching and gathering relevant information about the other party, their interests, and potential alternatives. Set clear objectives and define your own interests and priorities. 2. Active Listening: Actively listen to the other party's perspective, concerns, and interests. Seek to understand their underlying motivations and goals. Ask open-ended questions and practice empathy to build rapport. 3. Effective Communication: Clearly articulate your own position, needs, and preferences. Use persuasive language, logical reasoning, and evidence to support your proposals. Be concise and avoid misunderstandings. 4. Problem-Solving Mindset: Approach negotiations as a problem-solving exercise rather than a win-lose situation. Look for common ground and explore creative solutions that address the interests of both parties. 5. Flexibility: Be open to compromise and explore alternative options. Consider trade-offs that can meet the needs of both parties. Maintain a cooperative attitude and be willing to adjust your position to find a mutually beneficial outcome. 6. Building Relationships: Focus on building trust and establishing a good rapport with the other party. Seek to understand their perspective and find shared interests. Emphasize long-term relationships and mutual benefits. 7. Patience and Perseverance: Negotiations can be complex and time-consuming. Be patient and persevere through challenges and setbacks. Maintain a positive attitude and be willing to explore different approaches. 8. Seek Win-Win Solutions: Aim for outcomes where both parties feel

satisfied and their interests are met. Look for opportunities to expand the value and benefits of the agreement. Avoid zero-sum thinking where one party's gain is perceived as the other's loss.

BENEFITS OF SUCCESSFUL NEGOTIATION

Effective negotiation skills can bring several benefits to businesses, including: 1. Successful Partnerships: Negotiating fair and mutually beneficial agreements with business partners can lead to long-lasting and profitable partnerships. 2. Cost Savings: Skilled negotiators can secure favorable terms and conditions, leading to reduced costs and increased profitability. 3. Conflict Resolution: Negotiation is a key tool for resolving conflicts and disputes between parties, saving time and resources. 4. Enhanced Relationships: Successful negotiation fosters trust and collaboration, strengthening relationships with customers, suppliers, and stakeholders. 5. Competitive Advantage: Businesses with strong negotiation skills have a competitive edge in securing favorable deals and navigating challenging situations.

CONCLUSION

The Law of Negotiation highlights the importance of effective communication, strategic thinking, and finding mutually beneficial solutions. By developing negotiation skills and applying key strategies, businesses can achieve successful outcomes, build strong relationships, and gain a competitive advantage in the marketplace.

Chapter 22: The Rule of Risk Management

Risk management is a fundamental aspect of running a successful business. The Rule of Risk Management emphasizes the importance of identifying, assessing, and mitigating risks to minimize potential negative impacts on the business.

THE IMPORTANCE OF RISK MANAGEMENT IN BUSINESS

Effective risk management allows businesses to proactively identify potential hazards, make informed decisions, and implement strategies to prevent or reduce the likelihood of negative outcomes. It helps safeguard the business's reputation, protects assets, ensures compliance with regulations, and enhances overall business performance.

KEY PRINCIPLES OF RISK MANAGEMENT

To effectively apply the Rule of Risk Management, business owners and managers should adhere to several key principles: 1. Proactive Approach: Risk management should be an ongoing process that starts from the inception of a business and continues throughout its entire lifecycle. It involves anticipating potential risks and developing strategies to mitigate them. 2. Risk Identification: In order to manage risks, they must first be identified. This involves conducting a comprehensive assessment of all potential risks associated with the business's operations, such as financial risks, operational risks, legal risks, technological risks, and market risks. 3. Risk Assessment: Once risks are identified, they should be assessed based on their likelihood of occurrence and potential impact on the business. This allows the business to prioritize risks and allocate resources accordingly. 4. Risk Mitigation: After assessing risks, measures should be put in place to mitigate or minimize their potential impact. This can involve implementing control systems, developing contingency plans, diversifying business operations, and obtaining appropriate insurance coverage. 5. Regular Monitoring and Review: Risk management is an ongoing process that requires continuous monitoring and review. This ensures that risks are effectively managed and that new risks are identified as the business landscape evolves.

STRATEGIES FOR EFFECTIVE RISK MANAGEMENT

Implementing effective risk management strategies can help businesses navigate uncertainties and protect their interests. Here are some strategies to consider: 1. Establish a Risk Management Culture: Foster a culture of risk awareness and accountability throughout the organization. Encourage employees to report potential risks and provide them with the necessary training to identify and mitigate risks. 2. Develop a Risk Management Plan: Create a comprehensive risk management plan that outlines the strategies, tools, and processes for identifying, assessing, and mitigating risks. Define roles and responsibilities within the organization and establish clear protocols for reporting and addressing risks. 3. Conduct Regular Risk Assessments: Regularly assess and reassess risks to ensure that the risk management plan remains relevant and effective. Identify any emerging risks and update mitigation strategies accordingly. 4. Implement Internal Controls: Implement robust internal control systems to prevent and detect potential risks. This can include segregation of duties, regular financial audits, and IT security measures to protect against cyber threats. 5. Maintain Effective Communication: Open and transparent communication is key to effective risk management. Establish channels for reporting and discussing risks, and ensure that information flows freely across all levels of the organization. 6. Continuously Improve: Risk management is a dynamic process. Continuously monitor, evaluate, and improve risk management measures based on lessons learned and emerging best practices.

CONCLUSION

The Rule of Risk Management highlights the importance of proactively managing potential risks to ensure the long-term success and sustainability of a business. By implementing effective risk management strategies, businesses can identify and address potential hazards, protect their assets, and make informed decisions that minimize potential negative impacts. Embracing risk management as a core principle helps businesses navigate uncertainties and achieve their strategic objectives.

Chapter 23: The Law of Financial Planning

Financial planning is a crucial aspect of running a successful business. The Law of Financial Planning highlights the importance of effectively managing finances to ensure long-term stability and growth. By adopting sound financial planning practices, businesses can make informed decisions, allocate resources effectively, and achieve their financial goals.

THE IMPORTANCE OF FINANCIAL PLANNING

Financial planning is the process of setting financial goals, creating a roadmap to achieve those goals, and regularly monitoring and adjusting the plan as needed. It allows businesses to have a clear understanding of their current financial status, identify areas for improvement, and make strategic decisions to maximize profitability. Effective financial planning provides several benefits, including: 1. **Budgeting and cash flow management:** Financial planning helps businesses develop budgets and manage cash flow. It involves analyzing income and expenses and ensuring that the company has enough cash to cover its obligations and invest in growth opportunities. 2. **Resource allocation:** Financial planning allows businesses to allocate resources optimally. By understanding their financial situation and goals, businesses can prioritize investments, expenses, and operational needs. 3. **Risk management:** Financial planning helps businesses identify and manage financial risks. By conducting risk assessments and developing contingency plans, businesses can minimize the impact of unforeseen events or market fluctuations on their financial health. 4. **Growth and expansion:** Financial planning plays a crucial role in business growth and expansion. It helps businesses determine the financial feasibility of expansion projects, assess financing options, and develop strategies to support growth while maintaining financial stability. 5. **Decision making:** Financial planning provides businesses with the information and insights needed to make informed decisions. It involves analyzing financial data, conducting cost-benefit analyses, and evaluating potential risks and rewards.

STEPS IN FINANCIAL PLANNING

Effective financial planning encompasses several steps: 1. **Establishing financial goals:** Businesses need to define their long-term and short-term financial goals. These goals may include increasing profitability, improving cash flow, reducing debt, or expanding into new markets. 2. **Assessing the current financial situation:** Businesses must conduct a comprehensive analysis of their current financial position. This includes reviewing financial statements, cash flow records, and other relevant financial data. 3. **Identifying financial strategies:** Once businesses have a clear understanding of their goals and current position, they can develop strategies to achieve those goals. These strategies may include cost-cutting measures, investment opportunities, debt management, or revenue growth initiatives. 4. **Creating a financial plan:** Businesses need to create a detailed financial plan that outlines the strategies, actions, and timelines required to achieve their financial goals. The plan should include budget forecasts, investment strategies, risk assessments, and key performance indicators. 5. **Implementation and monitoring:** Business owners and financial managers need to implement the financial plan and continuously monitor its progress. Regular monitoring allows businesses to identify deviations from the plan and take corrective actions as needed. 6. **Review and adjustment:** Financial plans should be reviewed periodically to ensure their effectiveness and relevance. Business conditions and goals may change over time, requiring adjustments to the plan.

BEST PRACTICES IN FINANCIAL PLANNING

To effectively implement financial planning, businesses can follow these best practices: 1. **Engage financial professionals:** Businesses can benefit from the expertise and guidance of financial professionals, such as accountants, financial advisors, or consultants. These professionals can provide valuable insights and ensure businesses adhere to best practices. 2. **Continuous education and learning:** Financial planning requires staying updated on financial trends, regulations, and industry practices. Business owners and financial managers should invest in their financial literacy and seek opportunities for professional development. 3. **Regular performance monitoring:** Businesses should establish a system to regularly monitor their financial performance against the set goals and benchmarks. This allows for early identification of any discrepancies or areas that require improvement. 4. **Risk assessment and management:** Businesses should conduct a thorough risk analysis and develop risk management strategies. This involves identifying potential financial risks, creating contingency plans, and implementing risk mitigation measures. 5. **Collaborate across departments:** Financial planning should involve collaboration across different departments or functional areas within the organization. This ensures that financial considerations are integrated into decision-making processes throughout the business. 6. **Stay agile and adaptable:** Financial planning should be flexible to accommodate changes in the business environment. Businesses should regularly review and adjust their plans based on market conditions, industry trends, and internal factors. By implementing effective financial planning practices, businesses can improve their financial health, make informed decisions, and achieve long-term success. It is essential to prioritize financial planning and allocate the necessary resources to develop robust financial strategies that support business objectives and mitigate financial risks.

CHAPTER 24: THE RULE OF MARKETING STRATEGY

In today's highly competitive business landscape, having a well-defined marketing strategy is essential for success.

The Rule of Marketing Strategy emphasizes the importance of developing a strategic approach to promoting products or services, attracting customers, and building brand awareness. A strong marketing strategy enables businesses to effectively communicate their value proposition, differentiate themselves from competitors, and achieve their business goals.

Understanding the Rule of Marketing Strategy

Marketing strategy refers to the overall plan and tactics a business uses to reach its target market, promote its products or services, and achieve its marketing objectives. It involves carefully analyzing market trends, consumer behavior, and competitors to formulate a comprehensive plan that guides all marketing activities. The Rule of Marketing Strategy encompasses several key principles that businesses should consider when developing their strategies: 1. **Market Analysis:** Before creating a marketing strategy, businesses need to conduct a thorough analysis of their target market. This includes identifying customer needs, preferences, and behaviors, as well as assessing market trends and competitor offerings. By understanding the market landscape, businesses can tailor their marketing strategies to effectively reach their target audience. 2. **Segmentation and Targeting:** The Rule of Marketing Strategy highlights the importance of segmenting the market and targeting specific customer groups. By dividing the market into smaller segments based on demographics, psychographics, or buying behaviors, businesses can create more personalized and relevant marketing messages. This allows them to connect with their target audience on a deeper level, increasing the chances of attracting and retaining customers. 3. **Unique Value Proposition:** A strong marketing strategy revolves around developing a unique value proposition that differentiates a business from its competitors. The Rule of Marketing Strategy emphasizes the importance of clearly defining and communicating what sets a business apart and how it addresses customer needs better than alternatives. This unique value proposition forms the foundation of all marketing efforts and helps businesses attract and retain customers. 4. **Integrated Marketing Communications:** The Rule of Marketing Strategy advocates for an integrated approach to marketing communications. This means aligning all marketing activities and messages across various channels, such as advertising, public relations, social media, and content marketing, to create a consistent and cohesive brand image. Integrated marketing communications reinforce the brand message, increase brand awareness, and improve overall marketing effectiveness. 5. **Measuring and Evaluating:** The Rule of Marketing Strategy emphasizes the importance of measuring and evaluating the effectiveness of marketing initiatives. By setting clear marketing objectives and key performance indicators, businesses can track their progress and make data-driven decisions. Regular monitoring and analyzing of marketing metrics allow businesses to identify what is working and what needs improvement, enabling them to optimize their strategies for better results.

Applying the Rule of Marketing Strategy

To effectively apply the Rule of Marketing Strategy, businesses should consider the following strategies: 1. **Set Clear Objectives:** Clearly define the marketing objectives that your strategy aims to achieve. Whether it's increasing brand awareness, generating leads, or boosting sales, having specific, measurable, achievable, relevant, and time-bound (SMART) goals will provide focus and direction for your marketing efforts. 2. **Know Your Target Audience:** Conduct thorough market research to deeply understand your target audience's needs, preferences, and behaviors. This will enable you to tailor your marketing messages and select the most effective channels to reach them. 3. **Create a Compelling Value Proposition:** Develop a unique value proposition that clearly communicates why customers should choose your products or services. Highlight what makes you different and better than your competitors to attract and retain customers. 4. **Select the Right Marketing Channels:** Determine the most suitable marketing channels to reach your target audience effectively. This may include a combination of digital marketing channels (such as social media, email marketing, and search engine optimization) and traditional marketing channels (such as print ads, direct mail, and events). 5. **Develop Engaging Content:** Create high-quality and relevant content that resonates with your target audience. This includes blog posts, videos, infographics, and whitepapers. Engaging content helps build brand authority, attract traffic, and nurture leads. 6. **Implement Measurement and Tracking:** Establish key performance indicators (KPIs) and implement analytics tools to measure the effectiveness of your marketing efforts. Regularly review and analyze the data to identify areas for improvement and make data-driven decisions. 7. **Stay Agile and Adapt:** Continuously monitor market trends, customer preferences, and competitor actions. Be ready to adapt your marketing strategy as needed to stay ahead of the competition and meet evolving customer needs. By applying the Rule of Marketing Strategy and implementing these strategies, businesses can develop a strong and effective marketing plan that drives growth, increases brand visibility, and achieves their marketing objectives. **Conclusion** The Rule of Marketing Strategy emphasizes the importance of developing a well-defined marketing plan to effectively promote products or services, attract customers, and build a strong brand. By understanding the market landscape, defining a unique value proposition, using integrated marketing communications, and measuring the effectiveness of marketing initiatives, businesses can optimize their efforts and achieve sustainable growth. A strategic marketing approach is key to staying competitive in today's dynamic business environment. Next up is Chapter 25: The Law of Branding.

Chapter 25: The Law of Branding

Branding is an essential aspect of building a successful business. It goes beyond just creating a logo and a catchy slogan. The Law of Branding states that a strong and well-defined brand can have a significant impact on a company's success in the marketplace.

BUILDING A STRONG BRAND

To build a strong brand, businesses need to focus on several key elements. Firstly, it is crucial to have a clear and well-defined brand identity. This includes defining your brand's mission, vision, and values. Your brand identity sets the foundation for how your brand will be perceived by your target audience. Secondly, consistency is key. A strong brand maintains consistency across all touchpoints, from visual elements such as logos, colors, and fonts to the tone of voice and messaging used in marketing materials. Consistency helps to build trust and recognition among consumers. Another important aspect of branding is differentiation. Your brand should stand out from competitors and offer a unique value proposition. This can be achieved by identifying your unique strengths and communicating them effectively to your target audience. Furthermore, building a strong brand requires understanding your target audience. Conduct market research to gain insights into their preferences, needs, and desires. By aligning your brand with the expectations of your target audience, you can create a strong emotional connection and build brand loyalty.

THE POWER OF BRANDING

Branding has the power to influence consumer behavior and shape perceptions. A strong brand can create trust and credibility, which are crucial in building long-lasting relationships with customers. Effective branding also helps businesses to differentiate themselves from competitors. It allows you to communicate your unique selling points and establish a competitive edge in the marketplace. A strong brand can command a price premium and attract a loyal customer base. Moreover, branding extends beyond the products or services you offer. It encompasses the entire customer experience, from pre-purchase to post-purchase interactions. By focusing on delivering exceptional customer experiences, you can strengthen your brand and create brand advocates who will recommend your business to others.

BRAND MANAGEMENT

Brand management is an ongoing process that involves monitoring and maintaining the integrity of your brand. This includes ensuring consistent branding across all touchpoints, monitoring customer feedback and perception, and making adjustments when necessary. It is also important to protect your brand against potential damage. This may involve actively managing your online reputation, addressing customer complaints promptly, and taking legal action if necessary. Additionally, brand management involves continuously innovating and evolving your brand to stay relevant in a dynamic marketplace. This may include introducing new products or services, refreshing your brand identity, or adapting your messaging to reflect changing consumer trends.

CONCLUSION

The Law of Branding highlights the importance of building a strong and well-defined brand. By focusing on creating a clear brand identity, maintaining consistency, and understanding your target audience, businesses can harness the power of branding to influence consumer behavior, differentiate themselves from competitors, and build long-term success. Effective brand management ensures that your brand remains relevant and resonates with your target audience in a rapidly changing business environment.

Chapter 26: The Rule of Customer Service

Customer service is a crucial aspect of any business. The Rule of Customer Service emphasizes the importance of meeting and exceeding customer expectations to build strong relationships and foster loyalty. Exceptional customer service can differentiate a business from its competitors and lead to long-term success.

THE IMPORTANCE OF CUSTOMER SERVICE

Customer service goes beyond just answering inquiries and resolving complaints. It involves creating positive experiences for customers throughout their entire journey with your business. Providing outstanding customer service has numerous benefits: 1. Customer Retention:

Excellent customer service builds trust and loyalty, leading to repeat business and increased customer retention rates. Satisfied customers are more likely to become brand ambassadors and recommend your business to others. 2. Competitive Advantage: In a competitive market, providing exceptional customer service sets your business apart from the competition. It becomes a unique selling point and an important factor that customers consider when making purchasing decisions. 3. Reputation and Brand Image: Delivering excellent customer service helps develop a positive reputation for your business. Word-of-mouth referrals and positive online reviews can enhance your brand image and attract new customers. 4. Customer Satisfaction: When customers receive prompt, friendly, and helpful service, they are more likely to be satisfied with their overall experience. Satisfied customers are more likely to make repeat purchases and become loyal advocates for your brand. 5. Customer Feedback: Effective customer service allows you to gather valuable feedback from your customers. This feedback can provide insights into areas for improvement, new product or service ideas, and emerging trends.

STRATEGIES FOR EXCEPTIONAL CUSTOMER SERVICE

To apply the Rule of Customer Service effectively, consider the following strategies: 1. Training and Empowering Employees: Invest in training programs to equip your employees with the necessary skills and knowledge to deliver exceptional customer service.

Empower them to make decisions and resolve customer issues independently, within established guidelines. 2. Personalization: Tailor your customer service approach to meet individual customer needs and preferences. Use customer data and insights to personalize interactions and create personalized experiences. 3. Responsiveness: Promptly respond to customer inquiries, complaints, or feedback. Ensure that your customer service channels, such as phone, email, and social media, are actively monitored and responses are provided in a timely manner. 4. Active Listening: Practice active listening to understand customer concerns and needs fully. Allow customers to express themselves without interruption, and demonstrate empathy and understanding in your responses. 5. Consistency: Provide consistent customer service experiences across all touchpoints, such as in-store, online, or over the phone. Ensure that all employees are trained to deliver the same level of service and maintain consistent brand messaging. 6. Anticipate Customer Needs: Anticipate customer needs and proactively address potential issues before they arise. Be knowledgeable about your products or services and provide relevant information or recommendations to customers. 7. Compensation and Recovery: When mistakes happen, take responsibility and offer appropriate compensation or recovery solutions. This can help turn a negative experience into a positive one and rebuild trust with the customer. 8. Continuous Improvement: Regularly review and analyze customer feedback, metrics, and industry trends to identify areas for improvement. Use this information to refine your customer service strategies and processes continually.

CONCLUSION

The Rule of Customer Service emphasizes the significance of delivering exceptional experiences to customers. Exceptional customer service builds trust, loyalty, and customer satisfaction. By investing in training, personalizing interactions, being responsive, practicing active listening, maintaining consistency, anticipating customer needs, providing compensation and recovery solutions, and embracing continuous improvement, businesses can create a strong foundation for exceptional customer service, differentiate themselves from competitors, and achieve long-term success.

Chapter 27: The Law of Employee Motivation

Motivating employees is a fundamental aspect of running a successful business. The Law of Employee Motivation states that engaged and motivated employees are more productive, creative, and committed to achieving organizational goals. Motivated employees bring numerous benefits to a business, including increased productivity, improved job satisfaction, lower turnover rates, enhanced teamwork, and higher customer satisfaction. On the other hand, disengaged employees can have a negative impact on overall company performance. There are several key principles and strategies to effectively motivate employees:

1. RECOGNIZE AND APPRECIATE

Recognizing and appreciating employees' efforts and achievements is a powerful motivator. Positive feedback, praise, and rewards can boost morale and create a sense of accomplishment. Acknowledging employees' contributions fosters a positive work environment and encourages continued engagement.

2. PROVIDE MEANINGFUL WORK

Employees are motivated when they perceive their work as meaningful and valuable. Giving employees autonomy, responsibility, and opportunities for growth and development can lead to higher job satisfaction and motivation. Assigning tasks that align with employees' skills and interests ensures they feel challenged and engaged.

3. FOSTER A POSITIVE WORK CULTURE

A positive work culture is essential for motivating employees. Encouraging open communication, promoting teamwork and collaboration, and fostering a supportive and inclusive environment build strong relationships and boost employee morale. When employees feel valued, respected, and supported, they are more likely to be motivated and productive.

4. SET CLEAR GOALS AND EXPECTATIONS

Setting clear goals and expectations provides employees with a sense of direction and purpose. Goals should be specific, achievable, and relevant to both individual and organizational success. Regularly communicating goals and providing feedback on progress helps employees stay motivated and focused.

5. OFFER GROWTH AND DEVELOPMENT OPPORTUNITIES

Investing in employees' growth and development shows that the organization values their long-term success. Providing training programs, mentoring, and opportunities for promotion or advancement encourages employees to continually learn and improve their skills. When employees see a clear path for career development, they are more motivated and committed to their work.

6. FOSTER A HEALTHY WORK-LIFE BALANCE

Promoting work-life balance is crucial for preventing burnout and maintaining employee motivation. Encouraging flexible work arrangements, offering wellness programs, and promoting mental health support create a healthy and supportive work environment. When employees feel that their personal well-being is valued, they are more likely to be motivated and engaged.

7. COMMUNICATE AND INVOLVE EMPLOYEES

Effective communication is key to keeping employees motivated and engaged. Regularly sharing information about company updates, goals, and challenges helps employees feel connected and involved. Additionally, involving employees in decision-making processes and seeking their input shows that their opinions are valued and respected.

8. PROVIDE FAIR COMPENSATION AND BENEFITS

Fair compensation and benefits are important factors in motivating employees. Employees need to feel that their work is recognized and appropriately rewarded. Offering competitive salaries, performance-based incentives, and attractive benefits packages helps retain top talent and encourages employees to perform at their best. By understanding and applying the Law of Employee Motivation, businesses can create an environment that fosters engagement, productivity, and long-term success. Motivated employees are more likely to go the extra mile, collaborate effectively, and contribute to the overall growth and profitability of the organization. Next chapter: Chapter 28: The Rule of Performance Evaluation.

Chapter 28: The Rule of Performance Evaluation

Performance evaluation is a critical process in business that assesses the effectiveness and efficiency of employees' work performance. The Rule of Performance Evaluation emphasizes the importance of evaluating and providing feedback to employees to improve their performance, enhance job satisfaction, and drive organizational success.

THE IMPORTANCE OF PERFORMANCE EVALUATION

Performance evaluation serves various purposes within an organization:

1. Providing Feedback

Performance evaluations allow managers to provide feedback to employees regarding their strengths, areas for improvement, and progress towards goals. This feedback is essential for employees to understand their performance and make necessary adjustments.

2. Employee Development

Performance evaluations provide an opportunity for managers to discuss career aspirations, professional development goals, and training needs with their employees. This helps employees feel valued and supported, leading to increased motivation and productivity.

3. Goal Alignment

Performance evaluations ensure that employees' goals are aligned with the overall objectives of the organization. This helps in creating a cohesive and focused workforce, where everyone is working towards the same mission.

4. Identifying High Performers

Performance evaluations help identify high-performing employees who consistently exceed expectations. Recognizing and rewarding these individuals can motivate them further and inspire others to perform at their best.

5. Addressing Performance Issues

Performance evaluations provide an opportunity to address performance issues and develop a performance improvement plan if necessary. By addressing issues promptly and providing support, employees can have the opportunity to improve and contribute to the organization's success.

STRATEGIES FOR EFFECTIVE PERFORMANCE EVALUATION

To ensure that performance evaluations are effective and valuable, consider the following strategies:

1. Clear Evaluation Criteria

Establish clear evaluation criteria that are specific, measurable, achievable, relevant, and time-bound (SMART). This helps provide employees with a clear understanding of what is expected from them and how their performance will be evaluated.

2. Regular Check-Ins

Performance evaluations should not be a once-a-year event. Regular check-ins and ongoing feedback throughout the year are essential to track progress, address concerns, and provide support to employees.

3. Two-way Communication

Performance evaluations should be a two-way conversation between the manager and the employee. Encourage employees to provide their input, express their concerns, and ask questions. This fosters open communication and mutual understanding.

4. Professional Development Plans

Discuss professional development goals and create a plan with actionable steps to help employees enhance their skills and reach their career aspirations. This shows employees that the organization is invested in their growth and development.

5. Consistent and Fair Evaluations

Ensure that evaluations are conducted consistently across all employees and departments. This promotes fairness and helps in identifying areas of improvement and recognition.

6. Recognize and Reward High Performers

Acknowledge and reward employees who consistently perform at a high level. This can include bonuses, promotions, or special recognition. Celebrating achievements motivates employees and encourages them to continue delivering exceptional results.

7. Constructive Feedback

When providing feedback, focus on constructive criticism and specific suggestions for improvement. This helps employees understand their areas of development and motivates them to take action.

8. Follow-up and Accountability

After performance evaluations, follow-up with employees to ensure that mutually agreed-upon actions and goals are being implemented. Hold employees accountable for their commitments and provide ongoing support and resources for their success.

CONCLUSION

The Rule of Performance Evaluation highlights the importance of assessing employee performance and providing feedback to drive improvement and enhance job satisfaction. By implementing effective performance evaluation strategies, businesses can create a culture of continuous learning, development, and high performance, leading to increased productivity and overall success.

Chapter 29: The Law of Sales Techniques

Sales techniques play a crucial role in the success of any business. The Law of Sales Techniques emphasizes the importance of using effective strategies to close deals, build customer relationships, and drive revenue. In this chapter, we will explore key principles and strategies for mastering the art of sales.

THE IMPORTANCE OF SALES TECHNIQUES

Sales techniques are essential for converting leads into customers and driving business growth. Applying the right sales techniques can maximize sales potential, increase conversion rates, and foster long-term customer loyalty. By understanding and utilizing effective sales techniques, businesses can differentiate themselves from competitors, build trust with customers, and ultimately achieve sustainable success.

KEY PRINCIPLES OF SALES TECHNIQUES

1.

Active Listening

Active listening is a critical skill in sales. The ability to understand and empathize with customers' needs and concerns allows sales professionals to tailor their approach and offer relevant solutions. By actively listening to customers, salespeople can build stronger relationships and demonstrate their commitment to meeting customer needs. 2.

Building Rapport

Building rapport is essential for establishing trust and a positive connection with customers. Sales professionals should focus on creating a comfortable and friendly environment during sales interactions. This can be achieved by finding common interests, engaging in small talk, and showing genuine interest in customers' lives and experiences. Building rapport helps to build a strong foundation for a successful sales relationship. 3.

Effective Communication

Clear and effective communication is fundamental in sales. Sales professionals should strive to communicate their message concisely and persuasively. This includes using language that resonates with the customer, highlighting the benefits of the product or service, and addressing any objections or concerns. Additionally, nonverbal communication, such as body language and facial expressions, should be utilized to convey confidence and credibility. 4.

Needs Analysis

Conducting a thorough needs analysis is crucial for understanding the specific requirements and pain points of customers. By asking the right questions and actively listening to the responses, sales professionals can uncover the underlying needs and motivations of customers. This enables them to propose tailored solutions that address these needs and provide maximum value. 5.

Product Knowledge

Having in-depth knowledge about the product or service being sold is vital for sales success. Sales professionals should be able to confidently articulate the features and benefits of the offering, as well as address any technical or complex questions that customers may have. By demonstrating expertise, salespeople can instill confidence in customers and increase the likelihood of closing the sale.

STRATEGIES FOR EFFECTIVE SALES TECHNIQUES

1.

Create a Sales Process

Developing a structured sales process helps to streamline sales efforts and ensure consistency in approach. This involves defining the key steps from lead generation to closing the sale, and providing guidance on the techniques and strategies to be employed at each stage. A well-defined sales process allows for better tracking and analysis of sales performance, as well as continuous improvement. 2.

Build Trust and Credibility

Trust and credibility are crucial in sales. Sales professionals should focus on building strong relationships with customers based on honesty, transparency, and reliability. This can be achieved by delivering on promises, maintaining open and clear communication, and proactively addressing any concerns or issues. Building trust and credibility establishes a solid foundation for sales success. 3.

Adapt to Customer Buying Styles

Every customer has a unique buying style, and sales professionals should be adaptable in their approach. By identifying and understanding customers' preferences, salespeople can tailor their sales techniques to align with the customer's decision-making process. This may involve adapting the pace, level of detail, or communication style to effectively engage the customer and increase the chances of a successful sale. 4.

Handle Objections Effectively

Objections are inevitable in sales, and sales professionals should be prepared to handle them effectively. Instead of viewing objections as roadblocks, the focus should be on addressing them as opportunities to further understand and meet the customer's needs. By actively listening, empathizing, and providing relevant information or solutions, salespeople can overcome objections and move closer to closing the sale. 5.

Follow-up and Relationship Building

Following up with customers after a sale is critical for building long-term relationships and ensuring customer satisfaction. Sales professionals should nurture the relationship by providing ongoing support, addressing any post-sale concerns, and seeking feedback. Consistent communication and personalized follow-ups demonstrate care and commitment towards the customer, fostering loyalty and potential for future business opportunities.

CONCLUSION

The Law of Sales Techniques highlights the significance of effective sales strategies in driving business success. By applying active listening, building rapport, effective communication, conducting needs analysis, and mastering product knowledge, sales professionals can enhance their selling capabilities and achieve outstanding results. Furthermore, creating a sales process, building trust, adapting to customer buying styles, handling objections effectively, and focusing on relationship-building can further amplify sales success. By embodying these principles and strategies, businesses can excel in their sales efforts and achieve their desired goals.

THE RULE OF CUSTOMER RELATIONSHIP MANAGEMENT

Customer Relationship Management (CRM) is a vital aspect of business that focuses on building and maintaining strong relationships with customers. The Rule of Customer Relationship Management emphasizes the importance of nurturing these relationships to drive customer loyalty, satisfaction, and ultimately, business success. Effective CRM strategies involve understanding customer needs, preferences, and behaviors. By gaining insight into their motivations and desires, businesses can deliver personalized experiences that exceed expectations and foster long-term loyalty. Here are some key principles and strategies to apply the Rule of Customer Relationship Management: 1.

Collect and Analyze Customer Data:

CRM starts with collecting and analyzing customer data to gain a deep understanding of their preferences, behaviors, and purchase history. This data can be gathered through surveys, interactions, social media, and website analytics. By analyzing this data, businesses can identify trends, patterns, and customer segments, enabling them to tailor their marketing efforts and customer interactions. 2.

Segmentation and Targeting:

Segmenting customers based on various factors, such as demographics, purchasing habits, and preferences, allows businesses to target their marketing efforts with precision. By understanding the unique needs of different customer segments, businesses can deliver personalized messages, offers, and experiences that resonate with each group. 3.

Build Strong Customer Relationships:

Effective CRM involves building strong, trust-based relationships with customers. This can be achieved through open and transparent communication, personalized interactions, and exceptional customer service. Businesses should strive to go above and beyond to meet customer expectations and address their concerns promptly and effectively. 4.

Utilize CRM Technology:

Implementing a CRM system can streamline customer data management, automate marketing processes, and enhance customer interactions. CRM technology enables businesses to track customer interactions, manage sales pipelines, and monitor customer feedback. It also aids in creating targeted marketing campaigns, managing customer support tickets, and tracking customer satisfaction. 5.

Create Loyalty Programs:

Loyalty programs are an effective way to incentivize customer loyalty and repeat purchases. By offering exclusive rewards, discounts, or VIP experiences to loyal customers, businesses can reinforce their commitment to customer satisfaction and build long-term relationships. Loyalty programs also provide valuable data and insights that can further inform CRM strategies. 6.

Proactive Customer Support:

Providing proactive customer support shows customers that their needs are a priority. Businesses should anticipate customer issues and reach out to address them before they become major problems. By staying one step ahead and being proactive in problem-solving, businesses can build customer trust and loyalty. 7.

Regularly Engage with Customers:

Regularly engaging with customers through various channels, such as email newsletters, social media, and personalized follow-ups, keeps the relationship alive. Businesses should provide valuable content, updates, and offers that are relevant and personalized to each customer's preferences and interests. 8.

Seek and Act on Customer Feedback:

Encouraging and acting upon customer feedback is crucial for continuously improving products, services, and customer experiences. Businesses should actively seek feedback through surveys, online reviews, and customer support interactions. They should also take swift action to address any issues or concerns raised by customers, demonstrating their commitment to customer satisfaction. By implementing these strategies and principles, businesses can establish strong, long-lasting customer relationships. A solid CRM strategy leads to increased customer loyalty, improved customer retention rates, and positive word-of-mouth referrals. Ultimately, effective CRM contributes to overall business growth and success.

Chapter 31: The Law of Productivity

Productivity is a crucial factor in the success of any business. The Law of Productivity states that the level of output or results achieved is directly related to the level of input or effort put in. In other words, the more productive you are, the more you can accomplish with the same amount of time and resources. Improving productivity is essential for maximizing efficiency, meeting deadlines, and achieving business goals. Here are some key principles and strategies to enhance productivity:

1. SET CLEAR AND MEASURABLE GOALS

Setting clear and specific goals is the first step towards improving productivity. Clearly define what you want to achieve, and break down your goals into smaller, actionable tasks. By having a clear roadmap, you can prioritize your tasks and stay focused on what needs to be done.

2. PRIORITIZE TASKS

Not all tasks are equally important or urgent. The key to productivity is identifying the high-priority tasks that contribute the most to your goals and focusing on them first. Use techniques like the Eisenhower Matrix to categorize tasks based on their importance and urgency. By prioritizing effectively, you can ensure that your time and energy are focused on the most crucial activities.

3. ELIMINATE TIME-WASTING ACTIVITIES

Identify activities that waste your time and drain your productivity. These can include unnecessary meetings, excessive email checking, multitasking, or spending too much time on unproductive social media scrolling.

Minimize or eliminate these distractions to reclaim valuable time and energy.

4. DELEGATE AND OUTSOURCE

Recognize that you can't do everything yourself. Delegate tasks to capable team members who can handle them effectively, freeing up your time to focus on more critical tasks. Consider outsourcing certain activities or hiring freelancers for specialized tasks that are not core to your business. Delegation and outsourcing help to distribute workload efficiently and ensure that tasks are done by those with the necessary expertise.

5. IMPLEMENT TIME MANAGEMENT TECHNIQUES

Time management is essential for productivity. Techniques like time blocking, where you schedule specific blocks of time for different tasks, can help you stay focused and make the most of your time. Establishing routines and sticking to them can also improve productivity by minimizing decision fatigue and creating a structured work environment.

6. STREAMLINE PROCESSES AND WORKFLOW

Analyze your business processes and workflows to identify areas that can be streamlined or automated. Look for redundancies, bottlenecks, or unnecessary steps that can be eliminated or optimized. By improving the efficiency of your operations, you can save time and resources, leading to increased productivity.

7. INVEST IN CONTINUOUS LEARNING AND SKILL DEVELOPMENT

Embrace a growth mindset and invest in continuous learning and skill development. Stay updated with industry trends, advancements, and best practices. Acquire new knowledge and skills that align with your business objectives. Continuous learning not only enhances your expertise but also improves your problem-solving abilities and efficiency.

8. CREATE A POSITIVE WORK ENVIRONMENT

A positive work environment plays a significant role in productivity. Foster a culture of trust, collaboration, and open communication. Provide opportunities for employees to voice their ideas and concerns. Recognize and reward hard work and achievements. By creating a supportive and motivating work environment, you can boost employee morale and productivity.

9. EMBRACE TECHNOLOGY AND AUTOMATION

Leverage technology and automation tools to streamline processes, automate repetitive tasks, and increase efficiency. Use project management software, communication tools, and productivity apps to enhance collaboration, manage tasks, and track progress. Automation frees up time and resources, allowing you to focus on more value-added activities.

10. TAKE BREAKS AND PRACTICE SELF-CARE

Productivity is not just about working harder; it's also about working smarter. Remember to take breaks and recharge. Research shows that regular breaks improve focus, creativity, and overall productivity. Prioritize self-care activities like exercise, meditation, and adequate sleep that contribute to your overall well-being and mental clarity. By applying the Law of Productivity and implementing these strategies, you can optimize your time and resources, eliminate wasteful activities, and achieve greater results with less effort. Productivity is a key driver of success in business, so make it a priority and reap the rewards of increased efficiency and accomplishment.

Chapter 32: The Rule of Decision Analysis

In the fast-paced and ever-changing business environment, decision-making plays a crucial role in determining the success or failure of a company. The Rule of Decision Analysis emphasizes the need for businesses to make informed and strategic decisions to achieve their goals effectively. Decision analysis is the process of evaluating multiple options or alternatives and selecting the most favorable course of action based on a thorough analysis of potential outcomes, risks, and benefits. By following this rule, businesses can minimize the impact of uncertainty and make decisions that align with their objectives and values.

BENEFITS OF DECISION ANALYSIS

Implementing the Rule of Decision Analysis provides several benefits for businesses: **1. Minimize Risks:** Decision analysis helps identify potential risks and uncertainties associated with different courses of action. By thoroughly evaluating these risks, businesses can make informed decisions that minimize potential negative outcomes. **2. Optimize Resource Allocation:** Decision analysis allows businesses to allocate their resources, such as time, money, and manpower, more effectively. By evaluating the potential outcomes and benefits of each option, businesses can prioritize and allocate resources to projects or activities that have the highest potential for success. **3. Enhance Strategic Planning:** Decision analysis aids in long-term strategic planning by considering multiple alternatives and their potential impacts. This approach allows businesses to assess the feasibility and expected outcomes of different strategic initiatives before committing resources. **4. Improve Decision-Making Process:** By following a structured decision analysis process, businesses can improve their decision-making process. This involves considering different perspectives, gathering relevant data, and evaluating the potential consequences of each decision. This systematic approach helps reduce bias and subjectivity in decision-making. **5. Increase Confidence:** Decision analysis provides businesses with a sense of confidence and assurance in their decision-making process. By objectively evaluating the potential outcomes, risks, and benefits of each option, businesses can make decisions with greater certainty and confidence.

PRINCIPLES OF DECISION ANALYSIS

To effectively apply the Rule of Decision Analysis, businesses should consider the following principles: **1. Define Clear Objectives:** Before beginning the decision analysis process, businesses must clearly define their objectives. This involves identifying what they want to achieve and the key criteria for evaluating potential options. **2. Gather Relevant Information:** Decision analysis relies on the availability of accurate and reliable data. Businesses need to gather relevant information and data from various sources to support the decision-making process. This may involve conducting market research, analyzing financial data, or seeking expert opinions. **3. Evaluate Potential Outcomes:** Businesses should assess the potential outcomes and impacts associated with each alternative. This includes considering both quantitative and qualitative factors, such as financial implications, customer satisfaction, market share, and long-term sustainability. **4. Consider Risks and Uncertainties:** Decision analysis requires businesses to identify and evaluate the risks and uncertainties associated with each alternative. This involves assessing the likelihood of potential risks and their potential impact on the desired outcomes. **5. Apply Decision-Making Tools and Models:** Various decision-making tools and models can assist businesses in analyzing options and making informed decisions. These tools include decision trees, cost-benefit analysis, scenario analysis, and sensitivity analysis. Choosing the right tool depends on the specific decision context and available data. **6. Involve Stakeholders:** Involving relevant stakeholders in the decision-making process can provide valuable insights and perspectives. This ensures that all relevant factors and considerations are taken into account before making a final decision.

STRATEGIES FOR EFFECTIVE DECISION ANALYSIS

To implement the Rule of Decision Analysis effectively, businesses can follow these strategies: **1. Develop a**

Decision-Making Framework: Establish a structured decision-making framework that outlines the steps, criteria, and tools to be used in the decision analysis process. This ensures consistency and clarity throughout the decision-making process. **2. Encourage Collaboration:** Foster a collaborative environment where team members can share their expertise and perspectives. Collaboration allows for a more comprehensive analysis of options and promotes collective decision-making. **3. Conduct Risk Assessment:** Identify and assess potential risks and uncertainties associated with each option. This involves considering both internal and external factors that could impact the desired outcomes. **4. Assess the Impact on Stakeholders:** Evaluate the potential impact of each alternative on relevant stakeholders, such as customers, employees, partners, and shareholders. This ensures that the decision aligns with the best interests of all parties involved. **5. Seek Expert Advice:** Consult experts or industry professionals who can provide valuable insights and expert opinions. Their expertise can enhance the decision analysis process and bring new perspectives to light. **6. Document and Communicate the Decision:** Clearly document the decision-making process, including the analysis, rationale, and outcomes of the decision. Communicate the decision to all relevant stakeholders to ensure transparency and alignment.

CONCLUSION

The Rule of Decision Analysis is a valuable tool for businesses to make informed and strategic decisions. By applying this rule, businesses can minimize risks, optimize resource allocation, enhance strategic planning, improve the decision-making process, and increase confidence in their decisions. Understanding the principles and strategies of decision analysis allows businesses to navigate the complexities of the business environment and achieve their goals effectively.

CHAPTER 33: THE LAW OF BUSINESS ETHICS

In today's business environment, ethics play a vital role in shaping the reputation and success of a company. The Law of Business Ethics states that businesses should operate with integrity, honesty, and fairness in all their dealings. It emphasizes the importance of ethical behavior in building trust with customers, employees, investors, and the broader community. Ethical business practices are not only the right thing to do, but they also have several benefits for businesses. Here are some key reasons why adhering to ethical principles is crucial: 1. Reputation and Trust: Ethical behavior builds a positive reputation for a company. Customers, employees, and stakeholders trust and respect companies that demonstrate ethical practices. This trust is essential for long-term success and establishing lasting relationships with customers and partners. 2. Customer Loyalty: Customers are more likely to support companies that prioritize ethical conduct. When businesses act ethically, customers feel confident about their decision to engage with the company and are more likely to become loyal advocates. Additionally, ethical companies tend to attract like-minded customers who align with their values. 3. Employee Engagement: Ethical behavior fosters a positive work culture and increases employee engagement. When employees feel valued and respected, they are motivated to perform their best and contribute to the overall success of the company. Ethical practices, such as fair compensation, equal opportunities, and transparency, create a sense of trust and loyalty among employees. 4. Legal Compliance and Risk Management: Adhering to ethical standards ensures legal compliance and minimizes the risk of legal issues. Ethical business practices involve understanding and following applicable laws and regulations. By integrating ethical considerations into decision-making processes, businesses can identify and mitigate potential risks before they become major legal or reputational problems. 5. Competitive Advantage: Ethical behavior can provide a significant competitive advantage. Companies that prioritize ethical practices create a unique selling proposition and differentiate themselves from competitors. Ethical conduct can be a key factor that differentiates a company when customers have multiple options to choose from. To ensure adherence to the Law of Business Ethics, businesses should consider the following strategies: 1. Define and Communicate Ethical Standards: Clearly articulating ethical standards and expectations is crucial. Businesses should develop a code of ethics or a set of guiding principles that outline the company's commitment to integrity, fairness, and ethical conduct. These standards should be communicated to all employees and stakeholders to ensure everyone understands the ethical expectations. 2. Foster Ethical Culture: Building an ethical culture starts at the top. Leaders should lead by example and demonstrate ethics in their actions and decision-making. They should promote open communication, support ethical dilemmas resolution, and create an environment that encourages ethical behavior. Regular training programs and workshops can

135

help employees understand the importance of ethics and provide guidance on ethical decision-making. 3. Ethical Decision-Making: Businesses should establish processes for ethical decision-making. Employees should feel empowered to raise ethical concerns and have access to channels for reporting unethical behavior. Having an ethics committee or a designated person responsible for overseeing ethical concerns can help businesses address and resolve ethical dilemmas effectively. 4. Supplier and Partner Selection: Businesses should extend their ethical considerations to their supply chain and partners. Conducting due diligence on suppliers and partners to ensure they align with the company's ethical standards is crucial. Collaboration with ethically-minded suppliers and partners can strengthen a company's ethical reputation. 5. Regular Ethics Audits: Periodic internal audits should be conducted to assess the company's adherence to ethical standards and identify areas for improvement. These audits can help identify any potential issues before they escalate and allow businesses to make necessary changes to strengthen their ethical practices. By adhering to the Law of Business Ethics, companies can build a strong reputation, foster trust among stakeholders, attract loyal customers, and create a positive work environment. Ethical behavior not only contributes to the long-term success of a business but also ensures its sustainability and positive impact on society.

Chapter 34: The Rule of Goal Setting

Setting goals is a fundamental aspect of business success. The Rule of Goal Setting emphasizes the importance of clear and well-defined goals to guide business strategies, actions, and decision-making. By setting goals, businesses can create a roadmap for success, align resources and efforts, and measure progress towards desired outcomes.

BENEFITS OF GOAL SETTING

Goal setting provides several key benefits for businesses: **1. Direction and Focus:** Setting goals helps businesses articulate their vision and mission, providing a clear direction for the organization. It helps focus efforts and resources towards specific objectives, avoiding distractions and maintaining a strategic focus. **2. Motivation and Engagement:** Goals create motivation and a sense of purpose for employees. Clear and challenging goals can inspire individuals and teams to perform at their best, leading to increased productivity, commitment, and satisfaction. **3. Measurement and Evaluation:** Goals provide a basis for measuring business performance and evaluating progress. They allow businesses to track key performance indicators (KPIs), identify areas of improvement, and make data-driven decisions. **4. Resource Allocation:** Goals help businesses allocate resources effectively. By setting priorities and identifying the most important objectives, businesses can allocate resources such as time, budget, and manpower appropriately to achieve desired outcomes. **5. Strategic Planning:** Setting goals is an integral part of the strategic planning process. It helps businesses assess their current position, identify gaps and opportunities, and develop strategies to bridge those gaps and seize the opportunities.

GUIDELINES FOR EFFECTIVE GOAL SETTING

To effectively utilize the Rule of Goal Setting, businesses should follow certain guidelines: 1. **Specific and Measurable:** Goals should be specific and measurable to provide clarity and facilitate tracking progress. For example, instead of setting a vague goal like "increase sales," a specific and measurable goal could be "increase sales by 10% in the next quarter." 2. **Achievable and Realistic:** Goals should be challenging yet achievable. Businesses should consider their resources, capabilities, and market conditions when setting goals to ensure they are attainable. Setting unrealistic goals may lead to frustration and demotivation. 3. **Time-Bound:** Goals should have a clear timeline or deadline for completion. This helps create a sense of urgency and provides a timeframe for monitoring progress. Breaking larger goals into smaller, time-bound milestones can also increase motivation and accountability. 4. **Aligned with the Business Strategy:** Goals should align with the overall business strategy and objectives. Each goal should contribute to the larger vision and mission of the organization. This ensures that efforts are focused on areas that are strategically important. 5. **Shared and Communicated:** Goals should be shared and communicated with employees and stakeholders. This fosters alignment, encourages collaboration, and increases accountability. Regular communication about goal progress and updates keeps everyone informed and engaged. 6. **Flexible and Adaptable:** Goals should be flexible and adaptable to changing circumstances.

Businesses should regularly review and reassess their goals, considering market trends, customer needs, and internal capabilities. Being open to adjusting goals allows businesses to stay agile and respond effectively to challenges and opportunities.

IMPLEMENTING THE RULE OF GOAL SETTING

To implement the Rule of Goal Setting effectively, businesses should follow a systematic approach: 1. **Assess the Current Situation:** Businesses should evaluate their current position, strengths, weaknesses, opportunities, and threats before setting goals. This analysis helps identify areas where improvement or growth is needed and sets a foundation for goal setting. 2. **Define Clear Objectives:** Businesses should define clear and specific objectives based on the assessment. Objectives should be aligned with the overall business strategy and address areas of improvement or growth identified in the assessment. 3. **Break Goals into Actionable Steps:** Breaking goals into smaller, actionable steps makes them more manageable and increases the likelihood of success. Businesses should identify the key actions and milestones required to achieve each goal. 4. **Assign Responsibility and Accountability:** Each goal should have a designated owner or responsible party. Assigning responsibility ensures that someone is accountable for driving progress and achieving the goal. 5. **Establish Tracking and Evaluation Mechanisms:** Businesses should establish mechanisms for tracking and evaluating goal progress. This could include regular check-ins, performance reviews, KPI monitoring, and feedback loops. These mechanisms allow businesses to measure progress, identify barriers or challenges, and make adjustments if needed. 6. **Celebrate Milestones and Achievements:** Recognizing and celebrating milestones and achievements along the way provides motivation and reinforces a culture of success. Acknowledging progress encourages continued effort and commitment. By applying the Rule of Goal Setting, businesses can create a clear roadmap for success, align efforts and resources, and motivate employees to achieve their objectives. It is an essential tool for strategic planning, decision-making, and business growth.

CHAPTER 35: THE LAW OF ADAPTABILITY

In the rapidly changing business landscape, the ability to adapt is crucial for long-term success. The Law of Adaptability states that businesses must be flexible and responsive to external factors, market trends, and customer needs in order to thrive. Adaptability allows businesses to stay relevant, gain a competitive edge, and seize new opportunities. By embracing change and proactively adjusting strategies and operations, businesses can navigate uncertainties and overcome challenges. Here are key principles and strategies for applying the Law of Adaptability: 1. Embrace a Growth Mindset: Adopt a mindset that views change as an opportunity for growth and improvement. Encourage employees to be open to new ideas and approaches. 2. Stay Agile: Build a culture of agility and resilience within the organization. Be willing to experiment, iterate, and pivot when necessary. Foster a work environment that encourages innovation and creativity. 3. Monitor Market Trends: Stay informed about industry trends, market demands, and emerging technologies. Regularly assess the competitive landscape and identify potential disruptors. Use this information to anticipate changes and proactively adapt strategies. 4. Customer-Centric Approach: Prioritize a deep understanding of customer needs, preferences, and behaviors. Collect feedback and gather insights to identify areas for improvement and develop new products or services that meet evolving customer demands. 5. Continuous Learning: Encourage continuous learning and development for employees. Provide training opportunities that enhance skills and knowledge, enabling the workforce to adapt to changing demands. 6. Build a Diverse Team: Foster diversity and inclusion within the organization. Embrace different perspectives and experiences, as they bring fresh ideas and approaches that can help navigate changes effectively. 7. Collaborate with Partners: Forge strategic partnerships and collaborations with other businesses or organizations. Pooling resources, expertise, and networks can lead to innovative solutions and shared success. 8. Plan for Contingencies: Develop contingency plans to mitigate risks and respond to unexpected events. Anticipate potential disruptions and have alternative strategies in place. 9. Foster Effective Communication: Establish clear channels of communication within the organization. Ensure teams are regularly updated on changes and developments. Encourage open and transparent communication to effectively share information and address concerns. 10. Monitor and Evaluate: Continuously monitor and evaluate the effectiveness of adaptations made. Assess the impact of changes on key performance indicators and adjust strategies accordingly. By embracing the Law of Adaptability, businesses can position themselves as agile and resilient entities in a rapidly changing business environment. The ability to adapt and evolve will enable businesses to survive and thrive amidst uncertainties and drive long-term success.

Chapter 36: The Rule of Innovation

Innovation plays a critical role in driving growth, gaining a competitive edge, and ensuring long-term success in today's business environment. The Rule of Innovation emphasizes the need for businesses to embrace innovation as a core principle and mindset. By continuously seeking new ideas, processes, and technologies, businesses can adapt to changing market demands, identify new opportunities, and stay ahead of the competition.

WHAT IS INNOVATION?

Innovation encompasses a wide range of activities, including process improvements, business model innovation, product development, and creating a culture of innovation within an organization. It involves thinking outside the box, challenging the status quo, and creating something new or improving existing solutions. Innovation is not limited to a particular industry or size of business – it can be applied to any aspect of business operations.

THE BENEFITS OF
INNOVATION

Embracing the Rule of Innovation offers numerous benefits for businesses: 1. Staying ahead of the competition: In today's rapidly changing market, businesses must continuously innovate to remain relevant and competitive. By introducing new products, services, or strategies, businesses can differentiate themselves from competitors and attract customers. 2. Enhancing the customer experience: Innovation allows businesses to identify and address customer pain points, deliver unique and personalized experiences, and exceed customer expectations. By understanding their needs and preferences, businesses can develop innovative solutions that solve their problems effectively. 3. Increasing efficiency and productivity: Innovation often leads to process improvements and the implementation of new technologies that streamline operations and eliminate inefficiencies. By identifying bottlenecks and finding innovative ways to overcome them, businesses can improve productivity and reduce costs. 4. Identifying new market opportunities: Innovation helps businesses identify emerging trends, market gaps, and untapped customer needs. By being proactive and forward-thinking, businesses can develop innovative products or services that cater to these opportunities, gaining a first-mover advantage. 5. Fostering a culture of creativity and learning: The Rule of Innovation encourages businesses to foster a culture that values creativity, risk-taking, and continuous learning. By empowering employees to generate and share ideas, businesses can tap into their collective intelligence and drive innovation from within.

STRATEGIES FOR FOSTERING INNOVATION

To effectively apply the Rule of Innovation, businesses can implement the following strategies: 1. Encouraging idea generation: Create an environment where employees feel empowered to generate and share their ideas. Establish channels for collecting and evaluating ideas, and provide incentives and recognition for innovation. 2. Investing in research and development (R&D): Allocate resources towards R&D efforts. This can involve hiring experts, conducting market research, exploring new technologies, and testing prototypes. 3. Embracing risk-taking: Innovation inherently involves taking risks. Encourage employees to experiment, learn from failures, and embrace calculated risks. Create a safe environment where mistakes are seen as learning opportunities. 4. Collaborating with external partners: Strategic partnerships, collaborations, and open innovation initiatives can accelerate the innovation process. Partner with other organizations, startups, or universities to access new perspectives, expertise, and resources. 5. Providing training and development: Equip employees with the knowledge, skills, and tools necessary for innovation. Provide training programs, workshops, and resources to foster creativity, problem-solving, and innovation-oriented thinking. 6. Establishing an innovation team: Designate a dedicated team responsible for driving innovation within the organization. This team can be tasked with generating ideas, conducting feasibility studies, piloting new initiatives, and overseeing the implementation of innovative projects.

MEASURING THE IMPACT OF INNOVATION

Measuring the impact of innovation is crucial to evaluate its effectiveness and ensure a return on investment. Key performance indicators (KPIs) can be used to assess the success of innovation efforts. Some common KPIs include: 1. Revenue from new products or services: Tracking revenue generated from innovative offerings can indicate the success and acceptance of these products or services in the market. 2. Customer satisfaction and loyalty: Monitoring customer satisfaction levels and measuring customer loyalty can provide insights into how well innovative solutions are meeting customer needs and expectations. 3. Employee engagement and satisfaction: Assessing the level of employee engagement and satisfaction can indicate the effectiveness of innovation initiatives in creating a positive work environment and fostering a culture of creativity. 4. Efficiency and productivity improvements: Measuring improvements in operational efficiency and productivity helps quantify the impact of innovation on business processes and resource utilization. 5. Market share and competitive advantage: Tracking market share and comparing it with competitors' performance can indicate the effectiveness of innovation in gaining a competitive edge and capturing market opportunities. By regularly evaluating these metrics, businesses can gauge the success and impact of their innovation efforts and make informed decisions to further enhance their innovation strategies.

CONCLUSION

Embracing the Rule of Innovation is vital for businesses to thrive in today's dynamic and highly competitive business landscape. By fostering a culture of creativity, investing in research and development, embracing risk-taking, and implementing strategies to drive innovation, businesses can position themselves for long-term success. Through innovation, businesses can meet evolving customer needs, drive growth, and maintain a competitive edge in the marketplace

Chapter 37: The Law of Succession Planning

Succession planning is a crucial process that ensures the continuity of a business beyond the current leadership. It involves identifying and developing potential successors for key roles within the organization. The Law of Succession Planning emphasizes the importance of having a well-defined plan in place to ensure a smooth transition of leadership and to mitigate potential risks.

KEY PRINCIPLES OF SUCCESSION PLANNING

1. Identifying Key Positions

The first step in succession planning is to identify the key positions within the organization that are critical for its success. These positions may include top-level executives, managers, or any other role that plays a strategic role in the company's operations.

2. Assessing Leadership Competencies

Once the key positions are identified, it is important to assess the necessary competencies and skills required to excel in those roles. This assessment helps in identifying potential candidates who possess the desired qualities or in developing existing employees to fill those positions.

3. Developing a Talent Pipeline

Succession planning involves creating a talent pipeline to ensure a pool of potential candidates for key roles. This can be done through various methods such as mentorship programs, training and development initiatives, or job rotation opportunities. By nurturing and developing internal talent, businesses can build a strong bench of potential successors.

4. Building Leadership Capabilities

Successful succession planning involves investing in the development of leadership capabilities. This may include providing leadership training programs, coaching, or mentoring opportunities to potential successors. Building a strong leadership pipeline ensures that the business has skilled individuals ready to step into key roles when the need arises.

5. Creating a Succession Plan

A comprehensive succession plan should outline the processes, timelines, and criteria for identifying and selecting potential successors. It should also include contingency plans in case of unexpected events or emergencies. A well-developed succession plan provides clarity and guidance during the transition of leadership.

6. Communicating the Succession Plan

Open and transparent communication is vital in succession planning. Employees should be made aware of the company's succession plans to ensure a smooth transition and to alleviate any uncertainty or concerns. Communication also helps in engaging employees and motivating them to strive for leadership opportunities.

STRATEGIES FOR EFFECTIVE SUCCESSION PLANNING

1. Start Early

Succession planning should ideally begin long before the need for a leadership transition arises. By starting early, businesses have ample time to identify and groom potential successors, allowing for a seamless and well-prepared transition.

2. Involve Stakeholders

Involving key stakeholders, such as senior leaders, board members, and potential successors, in the succession planning process fosters a sense of ownership and commitment. By seeking input from various perspectives, businesses can make more informed decisions and ensure a successful succession.

3. Regularly Evaluate and Review

Succession plans should be regularly evaluated and reviewed to ensure their effectiveness and alignment with evolving business needs. As the company grows and changes, adjustments to the succession plan may be necessary to address any gaps or emerging leadership requirements.

4. Encourage Cross-Training and Knowledge Transfer

Cross-training and knowledge transfer among employees play a crucial role in succession planning. By providing opportunities for employees to learn from each other and gain exposure to different areas of the business, businesses can develop versatile employees who are capable of taking on leadership roles.

5. Consider External Candidates

While developing internal talent is important, considering external candidates can bring fresh perspectives and new skills to the organization. A diverse mix of internal and external candidates ensures a well-rounded succession plan.

6. Monitor and Adjust the Plan

Businesses should regularly monitor and adjust their succession plan as needed. Changes in business strategy, market conditions, or internal factors may require modifications to the plan. Being agile and responsive to these changes ensures the ongoing effectiveness of the succession planning process.

BENEFITS OF SUCCESSION PLANNING

Continuity and Stability

A well-executed succession plan ensures continuity and stability in the organization, even in times of leadership transitions. This allows for the smooth operation of business activities and minimizes disruptions.

Reduced Risks

Succession planning mitigates the risks associated with sudden leadership departures or unexpected events. By having a pool of potential successors and a clear plan in place, businesses can quickly respond to any leadership gaps and maintain business continuity.

Talent Development

Succession planning provides opportunities for talent development and career growth within the organization. This helps in attracting and retaining top talent, as employees see a clear path for professional advancement.

Improved Employee Engagement

Employees who see opportunities for growth and advancement within the organization are likely to be more engaged and committed. Succession planning demonstrates a company's investment in its employees, which leads to increased motivation and loyalty.

Strategic Alignment

Succession planning ensures that future leaders align with the company's strategic goals and vision. By developing leaders internally and aligning their skills and competencies with the business's strategic direction, organizations can maintain focused and effective leadership.

CONCLUSION

The Law of Succession Planning highlights the importance of preparing for the future by developing a strong pipeline of potential leaders. By identifying key positions, assessing competencies, and establishing a clear succession plan, businesses can ensure continued success and growth. Implementing effective strategies and regularly reviewing and adjusting the plan will help organizations navigate leadership transitions with confidence and maintain long-term success.

Chapter 38: The Rule of Networking

Networking is a fundamental aspect of business success. It involves building and nurturing relationships with individuals who can provide support, guidance, and opportunities. The Rule of Networking emphasizes the importance of cultivating a strong professional network to enhance career growth and business development.

THE POWER OF NETWORKING

Networking opens doors to new possibilities and opportunities. By connecting with industry professionals, potential clients, suppliers, mentors, and peers, you can gain valuable insights, knowledge, and resources. Networking allows you to exchange ideas, collaborate on projects, and learn from others' experiences. It helps you establish your reputation, increase your visibility, and build a strong personal brand.

EFFECTIVE NETWORKING STRATEGIES

To make the most of networking opportunities, it is crucial to adopt effective strategies. Here are some key principles to consider:

1. Define Your Networking Goals

Before stepping into any networking event or activity, clearly define your objectives. Determine what you hope to achieve through networking, such as expanding your client base, building partnerships, or gaining industry insights. Having specific goals will help you prioritize your networking efforts and make meaningful connections.

2. Be Genuine and Authentic

When networking, it is essential to be yourself and establish genuine connections. People are more likely to engage with someone who is authentic and trustworthy. Show a sincere interest in others by actively listening, asking thoughtful questions, and offering support or advice. Building authentic relationships will lead to long-term connections and mutual benefits.

3. Attend Networking Events

Participating in industry-related events, conferences, trade shows, and seminars provides excellent networking opportunities. Take advantage of these gatherings to meet like-minded professionals, industry leaders, and potential clients. Prepare an introduction that concisely communicates who you are and what you do. Exchange contact information and follow up after the event to solidify connections.

4. Utilize Online Networking Platforms

In addition to physical events, online networking platforms like LinkedIn, industry-specific forums, and social media groups offer virtual networking opportunities. Join relevant groups, participate in discussions, and share valuable insights. Connect with professionals in your field, and engage with their content. Online networking allows you to expand your network beyond geographic boundaries.

5. Nurture Relationships

Networking is not just about making initial connections but also about nurturing and maintaining those relationships. Regularly follow up with your contacts, offer support, share relevant resources, and celebrate their achievements. Stay connected through emails, phone calls, or meetings. Building strong relationships is a long-term commitment that requires consistent effort and genuine interest.

6. Give Before You Receive

One of the fundamental principles of networking is reciprocity. Give before you expect to receive. Offer assistance, introduce your connections to relevant opportunities, or share valuable industry insights. By providing value to others, you build trust and credibility, which ultimately leads to reciprocal support and referrals.

7. Be Strategic in Selecting Networking Opportunities

Time is a valuable resource, so it's important to be selective in choosing networking opportunities. Invest your time in activities and events that align with your goals and target audience. Focus on quality over quantity. Attend events where you are likely to meet key decision-makers or individuals who can contribute to your professional growth.

8. Embrace Continuous Learning

Networking is not only about meeting new people but also about acquiring knowledge and staying updated with industry trends. Attend workshops, webinars, or seminars to enhance your skills and expand your industry knowledge. Engage in discussions, ask questions, and share your expertise. Continuous learning not only enriches your networking experiences but also positions you as a valuable resource within your professional network.

CONCLUSION

The Rule of Networking underscores the significance of building and nurturing professional connections in today's business landscape. Effective networking strategies can lead to new opportunities, enhanced visibility, and invaluable support. By adopting a proactive and strategic approach to networking, you can build a robust network that contributes to your success and the growth of your business.

Chapter 39: The Law of Emotional Intelligence

Emotional intelligence (EI) is the ability to recognize, understand, and manage our own emotions and effectively navigate and respond to the emotions of others. It plays a crucial role in business relationships and can greatly impact the success and productivity of individuals, teams, and organizations. The Law of Emotional Intelligence states that individuals and businesses who possess high emotional intelligence are more likely to achieve success, build strong relationships, and effectively manage conflicts and challenges. By understanding and applying the principles of emotional intelligence, business owners can create a positive and productive work environment, enhance teamwork and collaboration, and improve overall business performance. Emotional intelligence is composed of several key skills and attributes, including self-awareness, self-regulation, empathy, motivation, and social skills. Let's take a closer look at each of these components and how they contribute to the Law of Emotional Intelligence: 1. Self-awareness: This is the ability to recognize and understand our own emotions, strengths, weaknesses, and impact on others. Self-aware individuals are better equipped to manage their emotions and make informed decisions. 2. Self-regulation: It involves the ability to control and manage our emotions, impulses, and behaviors. Self-regulation enables individuals to respond to situations in a calm and constructive manner, even in high-pressure or stressful situations. 3. Empathy: Empathy is the capacity to understand and share the feelings and perspectives of others. It enables individuals to connect with others on a deeper level, build rapport, and respond to their emotional needs with sensitivity and understanding. 4. Motivation: Motivation refers to the ability to harness emotions and use them as a driving force to achieve goals, overcome obstacles, and persist in the face of challenges. Motivated individuals are more likely to be resilient and determined in their pursuit of success. 5. Social skills: Social skills are the ability to effectively communicate, build and maintain relationships, influence others, and manage conflicts. Individuals with strong social skills can navigate social situations with ease, collaborate with others, and build strong and productive networks. By developing and nurturing these emotional intelligence skills, business owners and individuals can benefit in several ways: 1. Enhanced leadership: Leaders with high emotional intelligence are more effective in inspiring and motivating their teams, communicating effectively, and fostering a positive work culture. They possess the ability to understand and meet the emotional needs of their employees, thereby increasing engagement and productivity. 2. Effective communication: Emotional intelligence enables individuals to communicate clearly, listen actively, and understand the emotions and perspectives of others. This leads to better collaboration, conflict resolution, and effective problem-solving. 3. Relationship building: Strong relationships are built on trust, mutual understanding, and effective communication. The ability to empathize and connect with others on an emotional level helps build strong and lasting relationships with customers, employees, and business partners. 4. Conflict resolution: Conflicts are inevitable in any business setting. However, individuals with high emotional intelligence can effectively manage and resolve conflicts by understanding the emotions and perspectives of all parties involved and finding win-win solutions. 5. Stress management: Emotional intelligence helps individuals manage stress by recognizing its symptoms, regulating emotions, and implementing coping strategies. This leads to better mental health, improved decision-making, and increased resilience in navigating challenges. In conclusion, the Law of Emotional Intelligence emphasizes the importance of developing and applying emotional intelligence skills in business. By recognizing and understanding our own emotions and those of others, business owners can create a positive work environment, enhance teamwork and collaboration, and improve overall business performance. Investing in emotional intelligence development is vital for achieving long-term success in today's dynamic and interconnected business landscape.

Chapter 40: The Rule of Conflict Resolution

Conflict is inevitable in any business environment. It can arise due to differences in opinions, goals, values, or interpersonal dynamics. However, managing conflict effectively is essential for maintaining a harmonious work environment, fostering collaboration, and achieving business goals. This is where the Rule of Conflict Resolution comes into play.

THE IMPORTANCE OF CONFLICT RESOLUTION

Conflict, if left unresolved, can lead to negative consequences such as reduced productivity, increased stress levels, decreased employee morale, and even a toxic work culture. On the other hand, if conflict is addressed and resolved in a healthy manner, it can actually lead to growth, innovation, and stronger relationships within the team. The Rule of Conflict Resolution emphasizes the need for businesses to address conflicts proactively and constructively. By implementing effective conflict resolution strategies, businesses can minimize the negative impacts of conflict and create an environment conducive to collaboration and teamwork.

STRATEGIES FOR CONFLICT RESOLUTION

1. Identify the Root Causes: It is important to understand the underlying causes of the conflict to effectively address and resolve it. This can be done by actively listening to all parties involved and encouraging open and honest communication. 2. Seek Common Ground: Look for areas of agreement and shared goals between the conflicting parties. By focusing on common interests, it becomes easier to find resolutions that benefit all parties involved. 3. Encourage Active Listening: Active listening is crucial in conflict resolution. It involves paying attention to what the other person is saying without interrupting, showing empathy, and seeking to understand their perspective. This can help create a foundation for effective communication and problem-solving. 4. Foster Collaboration: Instead of approaching conflict as a win-lose situation, encourage a collaborative mindset where all parties work together to find mutually beneficial solutions. This involves brainstorming ideas, considering alternative perspectives, and finding compromises that address the interests of all parties involved. 5. Mediation and Facilitation: In more complex conflicts where emotions are high or communication has broken down, consider involving a neutral third party to facilitate the resolution process. Mediators can help create a safe and constructive environment for open dialogue and guide the conflicting

parties towards finding common ground. 6. Establish Clear Communication Channels: Clear and open communication channels are crucial for resolving conflicts effectively. Encourage regular and transparent communication within the team, and provide opportunities for individuals to express their concerns and feedback. This can prevent conflicts from escalating and allow for timely resolutions. 7. Focus on the Future: While addressing past issues is important, it is equally crucial to focus on finding solutions and moving forward. Encourage the conflicting parties to focus on the future and how they can work together to prevent similar conflicts from arising in the future.

BENEFITS OF EFFECTIVE CONFLICT RESOLUTION

Implementing the Rule of Conflict Resolution brings several benefits to a business: 1. Improved Relationships: By addressing conflicts proactively and constructively, relationships among team members can be strengthened. This leads to better collaboration, increased trust, and a more positive work environment. 2. Increased Productivity: Resolving conflicts allows team members to focus on their work instead of being consumed by tension and negativity. This leads to improved productivity and efficiency within the organization. 3. Enhanced Problem-Solving: Conflict resolution encourages open communication, active listening, and collaborative problem-solving. This can lead to innovative solutions and improved decision-making within the business. 4. Retention of Talent: A positive work environment that effectively resolves conflicts is more likely to retain talented employees. When individuals feel heard and supported, they are more likely to stay with the organization and contribute to its success. 5. Stronger Organizational Culture: Implementing effective conflict resolution strategies helps shape a positive organizational culture. When conflicts are dealt with in a respectful and constructive manner, it sets a precedent for open communication, trust, and teamwork.

CONCLUSION

The Rule of Conflict Resolution highlights the importance of addressing conflicts in a proactive and constructive manner. By implementing effective conflict resolution strategies, businesses can minimize the negative impacts of conflict and create a harmonious work environment where collaboration and productivity thrive. By embracing the Rule of Conflict Resolution, businesses can build stronger relationships, improve problem-solving capabilities, and enhance overall organizational performance.

Chapter 41: The Law of Continuous Learning

Continuous learning is a key principle for personal and professional growth. The Law of Continuous Learning states that individuals and businesses who embrace lifelong learning are more likely to thrive and succeed in today's rapidly changing and competitive world.

THE POWER OF LEARNING

Learning is a continuous process that should be valued and prioritized. It allows individuals to acquire new knowledge, skills, and perspectives, which can be applied to improve performance, solve complex problems, and adapt to new challenges. Similarly, businesses that encourage and support continuous learning among their employees are more likely to foster innovation, increase productivity, and stay ahead of the competition.

CREATING A LEARNING CULTURE

To fully embrace the Law of Continuous Learning, it is important to create a culture of learning within an organization. This involves promoting a growth mindset, where curiosity, experimentation, and continuous improvement are encouraged and celebrated. Some strategies to create a learning culture include:

1. Provide Learning Opportunities

Offer employees various learning opportunities, such as workshops, seminars, webinars, conferences, and online courses. Encourage them to seek out new knowledge and skills that are relevant to their roles or future career aspirations.

2. Support Personal Development Plans

Encourage employees to create personal development plans that align with their career goals. Provide resources and support, such as mentorship, coaching, and access to learning platforms, to help them achieve their objectives.

3. Foster Knowledge Sharing

Promote a collaborative and supportive work environment where employees feel comfortable sharing their expertise and learning from others. Encourage knowledge sharing through team meetings, presentations, internal wikis, and online discussion boards.

4. Encourage Self-directed Learning

Empower employees to take ownership of their own learning journey. Encourage them to explore topics of interest, pursue certifications or advanced degrees, and engage in self-directed learning through books, podcasts, videos, and online resources.

5. Lead by Example

Leaders should be role models for continuous learning. By demonstrating a commitment to learning and openly sharing their own learning experiences, leaders inspire and motivate others to embrace a culture of learning.

BENEFITS OF CONTINUOUS LEARNING

Continuous learning offers numerous benefits for individuals and businesses:

1. Adaptability

Continuous learners are more adaptable and agile in response to industry changes and technological advancements. They are better equipped to navigate uncertainties and embrace new opportunities that arise.

2. Innovation

Continuous learners are more likely to think creatively, generate new ideas, and approach challenges from different perspectives. This fosters innovation within the organization and leads to the development of new products, services, and processes.

3. Improved Performance

Continuous learning enhances individual and team performance by improving knowledge, skills, and competencies. It allows employees to stay up-to-date with industry best practices and trends, leading to higher levels of productivity and efficiency.

4. Career Advancement

By continuously learning and developing new skills, individuals increase their competitiveness in the job market. Continuous learners are more likely to be considered for promotions, new opportunities, and leadership roles.

5. Employee Engagement and Retention

A culture of continuous learning fosters employee engagement and satisfaction. When employees feel supported in their learning journeys, they are more likely to stay with the organization, leading to higher retention rates and reduced recruitment costs.

6. Competitive Advantage

Businesses that prioritize continuous learning gain a competitive advantage. They can leverage their knowledgeable and skilled workforce to innovate, differentiate themselves, and adapt to changing market dynamics.

CONCLUSION

The Law of Continuous Learning emphasizes the importance of lifelong learning for personal and professional growth. By embracing a culture of continuous learning, individuals and businesses can stay relevant, innovative, and successful in a fast-paced and ever-changing world. Remember, learning is a journey, and embracing it will open doors to endless opportunities. So, keep learning, keep growing, and reap the rewards of continuous learning.

CHAPTER 42: THE RULE OF PROBLEM-SOLVING

Problem-solving is a fundamental skill in business that involves identifying and resolving challenges or issues that arise in daily operations. The Rule of Problem-solving emphasizes the importance of approaching problems systematically and strategically to find effective solutions. Effective problem-solving allows businesses to overcome obstacles, improve processes, and make informed decisions. It requires a combination of analytical thinking, creativity, collaboration, and perseverance. By following a structured problem-solving approach, businesses can navigate through complex situations and achieve desired outcomes. Here are the key steps and strategies for applying the Rule of Problem-solving in business: 1. Define the problem: The first step in problem-solving is to clearly define the problem and understand its underlying causes. This involves gathering information, analyzing data, and identifying the specific issue or challenge that needs to be addressed. It is important to be specific and precise in defining the problem to avoid confusion and ensure a focused problem-solving process. 2. Generate alternative solutions: Once the problem is defined, the next step is to brainstorm and generate possible solutions. Encourage a diverse range of ideas and perspectives from team members or stakeholders involved in the problem-solving process. Consider both conventional and creative solutions, as well as solutions that have been successful in similar situations or industries. The goal is to generate a variety of options to choose from. 3. Evaluate and select the best solution: After generating alternative solutions, evaluate each option based on various criteria such as feasibility, cost-effectiveness, long-term impact, and alignment with business goals. Consider the potential risks and benefits associated with each solution. Select the solution that is most likely to solve the problem effectively and align with the desired outcomes. 4. Implement the chosen solution: Once the best solution is selected, create a plan for implementing it. This involves defining clear action steps, assigning responsibilities, setting timelines, and allocating resources. Communicate the plan to relevant stakeholders and ensure everyone understands their roles and responsibilities. Monitoring and measuring progress is crucial to ensure the solution is being implemented effectively. 5. Evaluate the outcome: After implementing the solution, evaluate its effectiveness. Assess whether the problem has been fully resolved and whether the desired outcomes have been achieved. Gather feedback from stakeholders and measure key performance indicators to determine the success of the solution. This evaluation phase provides valuable lessons and insights that can inform future problem-solving efforts. 6. Learn and improve: Problem-solving is an iterative process, and continuous learning is essential for improvement. Reflect on the problem-solving process and identify areas for improvement. Capture lessons learned and document best practices to apply in future problem-solving situations. Encourage a culture of learning and innovation within the organization to foster continuous improvement. By following these steps and strategies, businesses can navigate through challenges, overcome obstacles, and find effective solutions. The Rule of Problem-solving empowers businesses to become adaptable, proactive, and resilient in the face of complex and ever-changing environments. Remember, problems are opportunities for growth and improvement. Embrace the Rule of Problem-solving as a valuable tool for success in business.

Chapter 43: The Law of Employee Engagement

Employee engagement is a critical factor in the success of any business. The Law of Employee Engagement emphasizes the importance of creating a work environment that fosters employee satisfaction, motivation, and commitment. Engaged employees are more productive, innovative, and dedicated to their work, which ultimately contributes to the overall success of the company.

THE IMPACT OF EMPLOYEE ENGAGEMENT

When employees are engaged, they feel a sense of ownership and pride in their work. They are motivated to go above and beyond their basic job responsibilities, resulting in higher levels of productivity and increased quality of work. Engaged employees are also more likely to stay with the company for a longer period, reducing turnover and associated costs. Furthermore, engaged employees are more likely to be creative and innovative.

They actively contribute ideas, solve problems, and seek opportunities for improvement. This heightened level of creativity and innovation can lead to the development of new products, processes, and services, giving the company a competitive edge in the market. Employee engagement also has a positive impact on customer satisfaction. Engaged employees are more likely to provide exceptional customer service, going above and beyond to meet customer needs. Their positive attitude and dedication result in satisfied customers who are more likely to become repeat customers and recommend the company to others.

STRATEGIES FOR EMPLOYEE ENGAGEMENT

To foster employee engagement, it is essential for businesses to implement strategies that promote a positive work environment and meet the needs of their employees. Here are some key strategies for promoting employee engagement:

1. Clear communication and goal alignment:

Open and transparent communication is crucial in fostering employee engagement. Employees should have a clear understanding of the company's mission, vision, and goals, as well as how their work contributes to these objectives. Regularly communicate company updates, provide feedback, and seek input from employees to ensure alignment and engagement.

2. Provide opportunities for growth and development:

Employees value opportunities for growth and advancement. Invest in training and development programs that enhance their skills and knowledge. Offer opportunities for career growth within the organization and provide clear career paths. Empower employees to take on new challenges, responsibilities, and projects.

3. Recognition and rewards:

Recognize and appreciate the efforts and achievements of employees. Implement formal recognition programs that celebrate individual and team accomplishments. Provide rewards and incentives that align with employee preferences and motivations. Publicly acknowledge employee contributions to foster a sense of pride and motivation.

4. Work-life balance:

Support a healthy work-life balance by offering flexible work arrangements, promoting a supportive and inclusive culture, and encouraging employees to take breaks and vacation time. Recognize the importance of employee well-being and create an environment that values work-life balance.

5. Employee involvement and empowerment:

Involve employees in decision-making processes and give them a sense of ownership in their work. Encourage autonomy, empowerment, and innovation. Create a culture that values and respects diverse perspectives and encourages collaboration and teamwork.

6. Fair compensation and benefits:

Offer competitive and fair compensation packages that align with market standards and employee contributions. Provide benefits and perks that address employee needs and preferences. Regularly review and update compensation and benefits to stay competitive and attract and retain top talent.

7. Regular feedback and performance management:

Implement a robust performance management system that includes regular feedback, goal setting, and performance evaluations. Provide constructive feedback and guidance to help employees improve their performance and reach their full potential. Recognize and acknowledge progress and achievements.

8. Promote a positive and inclusive work culture:

Create a positive work environment that values diversity, inclusion, and respect. Foster strong relationships, teamwork, and collaboration. Encourage open communication and create opportunities for employee engagement, such as team-building activities and social events.

MEASURING EMPLOYEE ENGAGEMENT

Measuring employee engagement is essential to determine the effectiveness of engagement strategies and identify areas for improvement. Various methods can be used to measure employee engagement, including surveys, focus groups, and one-on-one interviews. These tools can help gauge employee satisfaction, motivation, and commitment, as well as identify potential areas of concern and improvement.

CONCLUSION

The Law of Employee Engagement highlights the importance of creating a work environment that fosters employee satisfaction, motivation, and commitment. Engaged employees contribute to higher levels of productivity, creativity, and customer satisfaction. By implementing strategies that promote employee engagement, businesses can enhance their competitive advantage, attract and retain top talent, and achieve long-term success.

Chapter 44: The Rule of Strategic Planning

Strategic planning is a crucial process for businesses to set clear goals, define the roadmap to achieve them, and make informed decisions to drive success. The Rule of Strategic Planning emphasizes the importance of developing a comprehensive and forward-thinking strategy that aligns with the organization's vision and objectives. Effective strategic planning enables businesses to navigate through challenges, seize opportunities, and stay ahead of the competition.

THE IMPORTANCE OF STRATEGIC PLANNING

Strategic planning provides a foundation for business growth and long-term success. It involves analyzing the internal and external environment, setting clear objectives, and formulating strategies to achieve them. Here are some key reasons why strategic planning is essential: 1. Goal Alignment: Strategic planning helps align business objectives with the broader organizational vision. It ensures that all stakeholders are working towards common goals, creating synergy across departments and functions. 2. Direction and Focus: A well-defined strategic plan provides a clear direction for the organization. It establishes priorities and guides decision-making, ensuring that resources are allocated to activities that contribute to the overall strategy. 3. Anticipation and Adaptation: Strategic planning involves scanning the external environment for potential opportunities and threats. It enables businesses to anticipate changes and adapt their strategies accordingly, ensuring long-term sustainability. 4. Resource Allocation: By identifying strategic priorities, businesses can allocate resources effectively. This includes financial resources, human capital, and other assets. Strategic planning helps optimize resource allocation to achieve maximum efficiency and effectiveness. 5. Performance Measurement: Strategic planning sets benchmarks and performance indicators to measure progress towards goals. It allows businesses to track their performance and make necessary adjustments to stay on track.

KEY ELEMENTS OF STRATEGIC PLANNING

To develop an effective strategic plan, businesses need to consider several key elements: 1. Situational Analysis: Businesses should conduct a thorough analysis of the internal and external environment. This includes evaluating the organization's strengths, weaknesses, opportunities, and threats (SWOT analysis). It also involves examining industry trends, market dynamics, and competitor analysis. 2. Clear Objectives: Strategic planning requires setting clear, measurable, and achievable objectives. Objectives should be aligned with the organization's vision and mission, and should be specific, measurable, attainable, relevant, and time-bound (SMART). 3. Strategy Development: Based on the situational analysis and defined objectives, businesses develop strategies to achieve their goals. Strategies should consider market positioning, competitive advantage, product/service differentiation, and target market segments. 4. Action Plans: Strategic planning involves breaking down strategies into actionable steps, assigning responsibilities, and setting timelines. Action plans define how objectives will be achieved and provide a roadmap for implementation. 5. Risk Management: Strategic planning includes identifying and mitigating potential risks and uncertainties. Businesses should assess risks associated with the strategies and develop contingency plans to address them. 6. Monitoring and Evaluation: Regular monitoring and evaluation of the strategic plan is essential. Businesses should establish key performance indicators (KPIs) to measure progress and make necessary adjustments to stay on track. This includes reviewing and analyzing market trends, customer feedback, and internal performance metrics.

BENEFITS OF STRATEGIC PLANNING

Strategic planning offers numerous benefits for businesses. Some of the key advantages include: 1. Improved Decision Making: Strategic planning provides a framework for making informed decisions. It ensures that decisions are aligned with long-term goals and are based on a thorough understanding of the business environment. 2. Competitive Advantage: A well-developed strategic plan helps businesses differentiate themselves from competitors. It allows businesses to identify unique selling propositions, innovative approaches, and market niches that give them a competitive edge. 3. Enhanced Resource Allocation: Strategic planning optimizes resource allocation by aligning resources with strategic priorities. It ensures that resources are allocated to activities that contribute the most to the overall strategy, minimizing waste and inefficiency. 4. Adaptability and Resilience: Strategic planning enables businesses to adapt to changing market conditions and mitigate risk. It ensures that businesses have contingency plans in place and are prepared to navigate through uncertainties. 5. Stakeholder Alignment: Strategic planning facilitates alignment among stakeholders, including employees, customers, investors, and partners. It creates a shared understanding of the organization's direction and fosters collaboration towards common goals. 6. Long-term Sustainability: Strategic planning provides businesses with a roadmap for long-term sustainability. It helps businesses stay focused on their vision and mission, adapt to emerging trends, and seize growth opportunities.

CONCLUSION

The Rule of Strategic Planning emphasizes the importance of developing a comprehensive and forward-thinking strategy to drive business success. Strategic planning aligns business objectives with the broader organizational vision, guides decision-making, optimizes resource allocation, and enables businesses to adapt to changing market conditions. By embracing strategic planning, businesses can gain a competitive advantage, enhance

stakeholder   alignment,   and   achieve   long-term
sustainability.

Chapter 45: The Law of Corporate Social Responsibility

Corporate Social Responsibility (CSR) is the ethical and moral obligation that businesses have towards society and the environment. It is the recognition that organizations should not only focus on maximizing profits but also contribute positively to the well-being of their stakeholders and the communities in which they operate. The Law of Corporate Social Responsibility emphasizes the importance of businesses acting responsibly and ethically to create a sustainable and inclusive society. Implementing CSR initiatives benefits not only society but also the business itself. It enhances the company's reputation, builds trust and loyalty with customers, attracts and retains top talent, mitigates risks, and fosters long-term success. With increasing awareness and demand for ethical business practices, customers are more likely to support companies that align with their values. Principles of Corporate Social Responsibility: 1. Ethical Behavior: Businesses should operate with integrity, honesty, and transparency. They should adhere to legal and ethical standards and conduct their activities in an ethical and responsible manner. 2. Social Impact: Companies should consider the social and environmental impact of their operations. They should strive to minimize their negative impact and actively contribute to the well-being of society through initiatives such as philanthropy, community development, and environmental conservation. 3. Stakeholder Engagement: Businesses should engage with their stakeholders, including employees, customers, suppliers, communities, and investors. They should listen to their concerns, incorporate their feedback, and consider their interests in decision-making processes. 4. Sustainability: Companies should adopt sustainable practices that minimize resource consumption, reduce waste, and promote environmental conservation. This includes measures such as energy efficiency, waste management, and adopting renewable energy sources. 5. Diversity and Inclusion: Organizations should promote diversity and inclusion in their workforce, ensuring equal opportunities for all employees regardless of their gender, race, ethnicity, religion, or other characteristics. They should foster an inclusive and respectful work environment. Strategies for Implementing Corporate Social Responsibility: 1. Stakeholder Analysis: Identify and understand the needs and expectations of your stakeholders. This includes customers, employees, suppliers, communities, and investors. Engage with them to better understand their concerns and interests. 2. Ethical Supply Chain: Ensure that your supply chain adheres to ethical standards, including fair labor practices, human rights, and environmentally sustainable practices. Create policies and guidelines for supplier selection and regular audits to monitor compliance. 3. Environmental Conservation: Implement sustainable practices to minimize your environmental impact. Reduce waste, conserve energy, promote recycling, and explore renewable energy sources. Consider initiatives such as carbon offsetting or reducing greenhouse gas emissions. 4. Employee Volunteer Programs: Encourage and support employees to engage in volunteering activities. This can include paid time-off for volunteering, organizing volunteer events, or supporting employee-led initiatives that contribute to social causes. 5. Philanthropy and

Charity: Allocate resources to support charitable organizations or community projects that align with your company's values and mission. This can include financial donations, in-kind contributions, or employee volunteering. 6. Stakeholder Engagement: Involve stakeholders in decision-making processes and consult them on important issues. Seek feedback and incorporate their perspectives into your CSR initiatives. 7. Transparency and Reporting: Communicate your CSR initiatives and progress to stakeholders through regular reporting. This includes disclosing social, environmental, and governance performance, as well as highlighting achievements and areas for improvement. 8. Collaboration and Partnerships: Collaborate with other businesses, nonprofit organizations, and government agencies to maximize the impact of your CSR initiatives. Form partnerships that align with your purpose and leverage collective resources and expertise. By embracing the Law of Corporate Social Responsibility, businesses can contribute to a better world while simultaneously enhancing their own reputation and success. Acting responsibly and ethically is not only the right thing to do but also a sound business strategy in today's socially conscious marketplace. Next chapter: Chapter 46: The Rule of Decision Making

Chapter 46: The Rule of Decision Making

Effective decision making is essential for business success. The Rule of Decision Making emphasizes the need for businesses to make informed and strategic decisions based on careful analysis and evaluation. Making sound decisions involves considering various factors, weighing the pros and cons, and choosing the best course of action that aligns with the organization's goals and objectives.

CLEAR OBJECTIVES

The first step in effective decision making is to define clear objectives. This involves identifying what you want to achieve and setting specific, measurable, achievable, relevant, and time-bound (SMART) goals. Clear objectives provide a framework for evaluating options and making decisions that align with the desired outcomes.

GATHERING RELEVANT INFORMATION

To make informed decisions, it is crucial to gather relevant information. This includes conducting thorough research, collecting data, and seeking input from relevant stakeholders. By gathering information from various sources, you can gain a comprehensive understanding of the situation, identify potential opportunities and risks, and make more informed choices.

EVALUATING POTENTIAL OUTCOMES

The next step in the decision-making process is to evaluate potential outcomes. This involves assessing the potential benefits and drawbacks of each option and considering the short-term and long-term implications. It is important to consider the potential risks, costs, and benefits associated with each decision and weigh them against the desired outcomes.

CONSIDERING RISKS AND UNCERTAINTIES

Every decision comes with its own set of risks and uncertainties. It is important to consider and assess these risks before making a final decision. This involves analyzing potential obstacles, identifying potential bottlenecks or challenges, and developing contingency plans to mitigate risks. By considering risks and uncertainties, you can make decisions that are resilient and adaptive to changing circumstances.

APPLYING DECISION-MAKING TOOLS AND MODELS

Various decision-making tools and models can aid in the decision-making process. For example, using a decision matrix can help evaluate options based on specific criteria, and a SWOT analysis can help assess strengths, weaknesses, opportunities, and threats. By applying these tools and models, you can streamline the decision-making process and ensure a systematic and thoughtful approach.

INVOLVING STAKEHOLDERS

Involving relevant stakeholders is important for effective decision making. This includes seeking input and feedback from those affected by the decision or those who have expertise or valuable insights. By involving stakeholders, you can gain different perspectives, identify blind spots, and build consensus, ultimately leading to more effective and well-informed decisions.

COMMUNICATING DECISIONS EFFECTIVELY

Once a decision is made, it is crucial to communicate it effectively to relevant stakeholders. Clear communication ensures that everyone understands the rationale behind the decision, their roles and responsibilities, and any necessary actions. Transparent and open communication fosters trust, engagement, and alignment within the organization, facilitating successful implementation of the decision. By following the Rule of Decision Making and applying these strategies, businesses can make informed, strategic, and well-thought-out decisions. Effective decision making optimizes resource allocation, minimizes risks, enhances organizational performance, and ensures long-term success in a rapidly changing business environment.

Chapter 47: The Law of Investment

Investment plays a crucial role in the success and growth of businesses. The Law of Investment states that allocating resources strategically and wisely can lead to higher returns and long-term financial stability. It is essential for business owners to understand the principles of investment to maximize their resources and make informed investment decisions.

THE IMPORTANCE OF INVESTMENT

Investment involves the allocation of financial resources, such as money, time, and effort, with the expectation of generating a return or achieving a specific goal. Here are some key reasons why investment is important for businesses: 1. Growth and Expansion: Investment allows businesses to invest in new projects, expand operations, and enter new markets. By allocating resources in growth areas, businesses can increase their market share and revenue. 2. Innovation and Technology: Investing in research and development, technology, and innovation enables businesses to stay competitive and adapt to changing market trends. It allows for the improvement of products, services, and processes, leading to increased efficiency and productivity. 3. Risk Management: Investment diversification helps businesses manage risks by spreading resources across different assets or industries. By diversifying their investments, businesses can reduce the likelihood of significant losses due to market volatility or unforeseen events. 4. Strategic Partnerships: Investing in strategic partnerships or acquisitions can provide businesses with access to new markets, technologies, or expertise. Collaborating with other companies through joint ventures or mergers can create synergistic effects and enhance competitiveness.

PRINCIPLES OF INVESTMENT

To make effective investment decisions, business owners should understand and apply the following principles: 1. Risk and Return: The relationship between risk and return is a fundamental principle in investment. Generally, higher-risk investments have the potential for higher returns, while lower-risk investments offer lower returns. It is important to assess the risk tolerance of the business and carefully evaluate the potential return on investment. 2. Diversification: Diversifying investments across different asset classes, industries, or regions can reduce risk and increase the chances of positive returns. By spreading investments across various sectors, businesses can minimize the impact of market volatility and capture opportunities in different markets. 3. Due Diligence: Conducting thorough research and analysis before making an investment is essential. This involves evaluating the financial health of the investment opportunity, understanding market trends, assessing potential risks, and considering the track record of the investment provider. 4. Time Horizon: The time horizon for investment refers to the duration over which an investment is held. Different investment opportunities have varying time horizons and potential returns. Businesses should align their investment decisions with their long-term goals and consider factors such as liquidity needs and market fluctuations.

STRATEGIES FOR INVESTMENT

To effectively apply the Law of Investment, business owners can consider the following strategies: 1. Set Clear Investment Objectives: Define clear investment objectives aligned with the overall business goals. This can include objectives such as capital preservation, income generation, or long-term capital appreciation. 2. Seek Professional Advice: Engage with financial advisors or investment professionals who can provide guidance based on their expertise and market knowledge. They can assist in conducting due diligence, selecting suitable investment options, and monitoring performance. 3. Monitor and Evaluate Investments: Regularly review and analyze the performance of investments to ensure they align with the business objectives. Monitor market trends, economic conditions, and industry developments that may impact investment performance. 4. Stay Informed: Keep abreast of market news and trends, economic indicators, and regulatory changes that may impact investment decisions. Continuous learning and staying informed about investment opportunities and risks are crucial for making informed decisions. 5. Review and Adjust Investment Strategies: Regularly review and adjust investment strategies based on changing business and market conditions. This may involve rebalancing investment portfolios, reallocating resources, or exiting underperforming investments. 6. Consider Tax Implications: Evaluate the tax implications of different investment options and structures. Consult with tax professionals to understand the tax-efficient strategies available and optimize investment returns.

CONCLUSION

The Law of Investment highlights the importance of strategic resource allocation and informed decision-making in business. By understanding and applying the principles of investment, businesses can maximize returns, manage risks, foster growth and innovation, and ultimately achieve long-term financial success. Effective investment strategies can provide businesses with a competitive advantage and position them for sustainable growth in a dynamic and ever-changing market environment.

Chapter 48: The Rule of Time Management

Time management is a crucial skill for business owners and professionals alike. Effectively managing your time can lead to increased productivity, reduced stress, and improved work-life balance. The Rule of Time Management emphasizes the importance of utilizing your time efficiently and prioritizing tasks to achieve optimal results.

THE VALUE OF TIME MANAGEMENT

Time is a valuable resource that cannot be replenished. By implementing effective time management strategies, you can maximize your productivity and make the most out of your available time. Here are some key benefits of time management in a business context: 1. Increased productivity: Proper time management allows you to focus on high-priority tasks, ensuring that important work gets done efficiently. This leads to increased productivity and the ability to accomplish more in less time. 2. Reduced stress: When you manage your time effectively, you can minimize the feeling of being overwhelmed by having a clear plan and structure in place. This reduces stress and helps you maintain a better work-life balance. 3. Improved decision-making: With better time management, you have more time for thoughtful decision-making. You can weigh options, analyze potential outcomes, and make informed choices without rushing. 4. Enhanced efficiency: Time management helps you identify and eliminate time-wasting activities or unnecessary tasks. By streamlining your workflow and eliminating distractions, you can work more efficiently and with fewer interruptions. 5. Effective goal achievement: Proper time management enables you to set clear goals, break them down into manageable steps, and allocate the necessary time to work towards them. This increases the likelihood of achieving your goals within the desired timeframe.

STRATEGIES FOR EFFECTIVE TIME MANAGEMENT

To effectively manage your time, it is essential to implement proven strategies and techniques. Here are some practical tips to help you optimize your time and improve your overall productivity: 1. Set clear goals: Clearly define your short-term and long-term goals. This provides direction and helps you prioritize tasks accordingly. 2. Prioritize tasks: Identify the most important and urgent tasks and tackle them first. Use techniques such as the Eisenhower Matrix, Pareto Analysis, or time blocking to prioritize tasks based on their significance and impact. 3. Avoid multitasking: Multitasking can lead to decreased productivity and increased errors. Focus on one task at a time, complete it, and then move on to the next. 4. Eliminate distractions: Minimize distractions that can interrupt your workflow. Turn off notifications on your phone or computer, close unnecessary tabs and applications, and create a dedicated workspace. 5. Delegate and outsource: Identify tasks that can be delegated to others or outsourced to free up your time for more critical responsibilities. Effective delegation allows you to focus on high-value activities. 6. Use time management tools: Utilize technology and tools such as project management software, calendar apps, and task management platforms to help you stay organized, track deadlines, and manage your schedule effectively. 7. Practice time blocking: Allocate specific time blocks for different activities or types of tasks. This helps create structure and ensures that each task receives the necessary attention within a defined timeframe. 8. Take regular breaks: It is crucial to give yourself short breaks throughout the day to rest and recharge. Stepping away from work for a few minutes can actually improve focus and overall productivity. 9. Learn to say no: Prioritize your commitments and be selective about the tasks and activities you take on. Avoid overcommitting and learn to say no when necessary. 10. Continuously improve time management strategies: Regularly evaluate your time management strategies and identify areas for improvement. Experiment with different techniques and adjust your approach based on what works best for you.

CONCLUSION

The Rule of Time Management highlights the significance of effective time management in business. By implementing proven strategies, setting clear goals, prioritizing tasks, and eliminating distractions, you can optimize your time and achieve greater productivity. Remember that time is a precious resource, and managing it efficiently can lead to increased success, improved work-life balance, and reduced stress levels.

Chapter 49: The Law of Self-discipline

Self-discipline is a key attribute that separates successful individuals from those who struggle to achieve their goals. The Law of Self-discipline emphasizes the importance of developing and practicing self-control and willpower in business endeavors. It is the ability to stay focused, motivated, and committed, even when faced with challenges or distractions. Self-discipline plays a crucial role in various aspects of business, including time management, goal setting, decision-making, and personal development. By mastering self-discipline, business owners can improve productivity, enhance decision-making abilities, and achieve long-term success.

THE BENEFITS OF SELF-DISCIPLINE

Developing and maintaining self-discipline in business brings numerous benefits. Here are some key advantages: 1. Increased Productivity: Self-disciplined individuals have the ability to prioritize tasks, eliminate distractions, and stay focused on their goals. This allows them to accomplish more in less time and be more efficient in their work. 2. Improved Time Management: Self-discipline helps individuals manage their time effectively by setting clear priorities, planning their schedules, and avoiding time-wasting activities. This allows business owners to allocate their time to the most important tasks and achieve better work-life balance. 3. Enhanced Decision-Making: Self-discipline enables individuals to make well-informed and rational decisions. By practicing self-control, business owners can avoid impulsive actions and consider the long-term consequences of their decisions. 4. Consistency and Persistence: Self-disciplined individuals are more likely to stick to their goals, even in the face of challenges or setbacks. They are better equipped to overcome obstacles and persist in their endeavors, leading to greater success over time. 5. Personal Development: Self-discipline fosters personal growth and development. By consistently challenging themselves and pushing their limits, individuals can learn new skills, acquire knowledge, and become experts in their respective fields.

STRATEGIES FOR DEVELOPING SELF-DISCIPLINE

Building self-discipline is an ongoing process that requires dedication and practice. Here are some strategies to develop and strengthen self-discipline: 1. Set Clear Goals: Clearly define your goals and break them down into smaller, manageable tasks. Set realistic deadlines and track your progress regularly. 2. Develop a Routine: Establish a daily routine that includes specific times for work, breaks, exercise, and personal activities. Stick to this routine as much as possible to build discipline and consistency. 3. Eliminate Distractions: Identify and eliminate distractions that can derail your focus and productivity. Put away your phone, close unnecessary tabs on your computer, and create a quiet and tidy workspace. 4. Practice Time Management: Learn to prioritize tasks based on urgency and importance. Use time management techniques such as the Pomodoro Technique or time blocking to stay focused and accomplish tasks efficiently. 5. Practice Delayed Gratification: Learn to delay immediate gratification and prioritize long-term rewards. This involves resisting temptations and staying committed to your goals, even when faced with short-term challenges or temptations. 6. Practice Self-reflection: Regularly reflect on your actions and behaviors, identifying areas for improvement and self-discipline. Be honest with yourself and hold yourself accountable for your actions. 7. Seek Support and

Accountability: Share your goals and aspirations with someone you trust, such as a mentor, coach, or accountability partner. Regularly check in with them to update your progress and seek guidance and support when needed. 8. Practice Self-care: Take care of your physical and mental well-being to strengthen your self-discipline. Get enough sleep, eat healthy, exercise regularly, and manage stress effectively. By consistently practicing these strategies, you can develop and strengthen your self-discipline, leading to increased productivity, better decision-making, and greater success in your business endeavors. In conclusion, the Law of Self-discipline underscores the importance of developing and practicing self-control and willpower in business. Building self-discipline brings a wide range of benefits, including increased productivity, improved time management, enhanced decision-making, consistency, and personal growth. By implementing strategies to develop self-discipline, business owners can unlock their full potential and achieve long-term success.

Chapter 50: The Rule of Personal Branding

Personal branding is a critical aspect of business success in today's competitive marketplace. It involves creating and promoting a unique and authentic image and reputation for oneself. The Rule of Personal Branding emphasizes the importance of developing and maintaining a strong personal brand to establish credibility, attract opportunities, and stand out in the crowded business landscape.

UNDERSTANDING PERSONAL BRANDING

Personal branding is about showcasing your expertise, values, and unique qualities in a way that resonates with your target audience. It helps you differentiate yourself from others and position yourself as a trusted authority in your field. Your personal brand reflects who you are, what you stand for, and what you bring to the table. It encompasses your professional reputation, online presence, communication style, and overall image.

Why Personal Branding Matters

Building a strong personal brand offers several benefits. Firstly, it establishes credibility and trust. When you have a well-defined personal brand, it becomes easier for others to know, like, and trust you. You become known for your expertise and can attract clients, collaborations, and career opportunities. Secondly, personal branding helps you stand out in a crowded market. By showcasing your unique qualities and sharing your insights and perspectives, you differentiate yourself from your competitors. This allows you to attract your ideal clients and partners who resonate with your brand. Moreover, personal branding creates a platform for thought leadership. When you consistently share valuable content, insights, and expertise, you position yourself as an authority in your industry. This can open doors to speaking engagements, media opportunities, and collaborations with other industry leaders.

DEVELOPING YOUR PERSONAL BRAND

To develop an effective personal brand, you need to start by understanding your strengths, values, and target audience. Here are some key steps to follow:

1. Define Your Unique Value Proposition

Identify what sets you apart from others in your field. What are your unique strengths, skills, and experiences? What value do you bring to your clients or customers? Having a clear and compelling value proposition is essential in attracting your target audience.

2. Identify Your Target Audience

Determine who your ideal clients or customers are. What are their needs, challenges, and aspirations? By understanding your target audience, you can tailor your messaging and content to resonate with them.

3. Build an Authentic Online Presence

Create a professional and consistent online presence through platforms such as LinkedIn, your personal website, and social media. Ensure that your profile reflects your personal brand and showcases your expertise. Share valuable content, engage with your audience, and maintain a consistent tone and visual identity.

4. Cultivate Thought Leadership

Establish yourself as a thought leader in your industry by consistently providing valuable insights and sharing your expertise. Publish articles, contribute to industry publications, and speak at conferences or webinars. This positions you as an authority and helps build trust with your audience.

5. Network and Collaborate

Build relationships with other professionals in your field and beyond. Networking allows you to expand your reach, gain new perspectives, and uncover partnership opportunities. Collaborating with others can further strengthen your personal brand and expose you to new audiences.

MAINTAINING AND EVOLVING YOUR PERSONAL BRAND

Personal branding is an ongoing process that requires consistent effort and adaptability. As you progress in your career or business, it's important to revisit and refine your personal brand. Here are some strategies for maintaining and evolving your personal brand:

1. Stay Relevant

Keep up with industry trends, advancements, and changes. Continuously update your knowledge and skills to stay ahead of the curve. This demonstrates your commitment to growth and adaptation.

2. Seek Feedback

Regularly seek feedback from clients, colleagues, and mentors. Understand how your personal brand is perceived and make adjustments accordingly. Actively listen to your audience and address any concerns or gaps in your brand.

3. Monitor Your Online Presence

Regularly review and manage your online presence. Ensure that your profiles and content align with your personal brand. Respond promptly to comments and messages to maintain a positive online reputation.

4. Embrace Authenticity

Authenticity is key to building a strong personal brand. Be true to yourself and communicate in a genuine and consistent manner. Share your successes, as well as challenges and lessons learned. Embrace vulnerability and connect with your audience on a human level.

5. Evolve with Intention

As your goals and interests evolve, be intentional about aligning your personal brand with these changes. Continuously assess whether your personal brand accurately reflects who you are and where you want to go. Don't be afraid to pivot or refine your brand as needed.

CONCLUSION

The Rule of Personal Branding underscores the significance of developing an authentic and compelling personal brand. Building a strong personal brand allows you to establish credibility, stand out in the market, and attract opportunities that align with your goals. By understanding and embracing personal branding principles, you can take control of your professional reputation and create a lasting impact in your industry.

The Law of Networking

In the business world, networking is not just a social activity, but a vital tool for success. The Law of Networking emphasizes the importance of building relationships, expanding connections, and fostering collaboration. Effective networking allows businesses to access new opportunities, gain industry knowledge, and establish a strong support system. Networking involves connecting with individuals who can offer valuable insights, resources, or partnerships. By building a diverse network, business owners can tap into a wide range of expertise, experience, and perspectives. Networking plays a crucial role in career advancement and business growth.

It allows professionals to stay informed about industry trends, market changes, and emerging technologies. Additionally, networking provides access to potential mentors, investors, clients, and partners. Strategies for effective networking include:

DEFINE NETWORKING GOALS

Before diving into networking activities, it's important to define specific goals. Whether it's expanding your client base, seeking career advancement opportunities, or finding potential partners, having clear objectives will guide your networking efforts.

BE GENUINE AND AUTHENTIC

Authenticity plays a key role in building meaningful relationships. People are more likely to connect with individuals who are genuine, trustworthy, and transparent. Approach networking with a mindset of building mutually beneficial connections, rather than solely focusing on personal gain.

ATTEND NETWORKING EVENTS

Networking events provide a valuable platform to meet like-minded professionals and industry leaders. Attend conferences, seminars, trade shows, and local meetups to expand your network. Make the most of these opportunities by actively engaging in conversations, exchanging business cards, and following up with potential contacts.

UTILIZE ONLINE NETWORKING PLATFORMS

In today's digital age, online networking platforms have become essential tools. LinkedIn, for example, allows professionals to connect with individuals in their industry, join relevant groups, and share insights. Engage in online discussions, offer valuable input, and use these platforms to expand your network globally.

NURTURE RELATIONSHIPS

Networking is not a one-time event, but an ongoing process. Nurture your connections by staying in touch, offering support, and providing value. Regularly check in with your network, offer congratulations on achievements, and provide assistance whenever possible. Building strong relationships requires time and effort.

GIVE BEFORE YOU RECEIVE

Networking is not just about what you can gain, but also what you can offer. Be generous with your time, expertise, and resources. Helping others without expecting anything in return can create a positive impression and strengthen your network. It fosters goodwill and reciprocity, leading to potential opportunities in the future.

BE STRATEGIC IN SELECTING NETWORKING OPPORTUNITIES

While it's important to network broadly, also be selective in choosing networking opportunities. Focus on events and platforms that align with your goals and target audience. Consider attending industry-specific conferences, joining professional organizations, or participating in niche communities where you can have the most impact.

EMBRACE CONTINUOUS LEARNING

Networking goes hand in hand with continuous learning. Stay updated on industry trends, emerging technologies, and new developments. Engage in professional development opportunities, attend workshops or webinars, and seek out mentors who can offer guidance and insights in your field of expertise. Networking is a powerful tool for individuals and businesses alike. By actively participating in networking activities, you can expand your knowledge, gain access to new opportunities, and build a strong support system. Remember, networking is an investment that requires time, effort, and authenticity.

Embrace the Law of Networking and discover the endless possibilities it can bring to your professional journey.

Chapter 52: The Rule of Effective Communication

Effective communication is a crucial aspect of running a successful business. It plays a significant role in building relationships, resolving conflicts, and ensuring that information is conveyed accurately and efficiently. The Rule of Effective Communication emphasizes the importance of clear and concise communication in all business interactions.

THE POWER OF CLEAR COMMUNICATION

Clear communication is the foundation of effective business operations. It enables employees to understand their roles and responsibilities, helps customers understand products and services, and fosters collaboration among team members. Clear communication also minimizes misunderstandings and ensures that everyone is on the same page.

Benefits of Effective Communication:

There are numerous benefits to practicing effective communication in a business: 1. Improved Collaboration:

When team members communicate effectively, they can work together more efficiently, solve problems, and achieve shared goals. 2. Enhanced Productivity: Clear communication ensures that tasks and deadlines are understood, reducing the likelihood of errors or delays. 3. Stronger Relationships: Effective communication fosters trust and transparency, leading to stronger relationships with employees, customers, and partners. 4. Conflict Resolution: By communicating openly and honestly, conflicts can be identified and resolved in a timely and constructive manner. 5. Customer Satisfaction: Clear communication ensures that customers' needs and expectations are understood, leading to higher levels of customer satisfaction.

Key Principles of Effective Communication:

To achieve effective communication, it is essential to follow these key principles: 1. Clarity: Messages should be clear, concise, and easily understood by the intended recipients. 2. Active Listening: Actively listen to others, ensuring that their perspectives and concerns are heard and acknowledged. 3. Nonverbal Communication: Pay attention to nonverbal cues such as body language, facial expressions, and tone of voice, as they often convey valuable information. 4. Empathy: Show empathy and understanding towards others' viewpoints and emotions, fostering a positive and supportive communication environment. 5. Two-Way Communication: Encourage open dialogue and feedback, allowing for a two-way flow of information.

Strategies for Effective Communication:

Implementing these strategies can significantly enhance communication effectiveness: 1. Choose the Right Channel: Use the appropriate communication channel based on the nature and urgency of the message (e.g., email, phone call, face-to-face). 2. Be Clear and Concise: Use simple and straightforward language to convey messages without unnecessary jargon or complexity. 3. Use Visual Aids: Support verbal communication with visual aids such as charts, diagrams, or presentations to enhance understanding. 4. Active Listening: Listen actively and attentively, asking clarifying questions and paraphrasing to ensure full comprehension. 5. Provide Feedback: Offer constructive feedback to colleagues and team members, recognizing their strengths and suggesting areas for improvement. 6. Adapt to Different Communication Styles: Understand that individuals may have different communication preferences and adapt your approach accordingly. 7. Be Respectful: Treat others with respect and professionalism, even during challenging or conflicting conversations. 8. Foster a Culture of Open Communication: Cultivate an environment where individuals feel comfortable sharing ideas, concerns, and feedback without fear of judgment or retribution. By following these principles and implementing effective communication strategies, businesses can optimize their operations, foster strong relationships, and drive success.

CONCLUSION

The Rule of Effective Communication emphasizes the importance of clear and concise communication in all aspects of business. By practicing effective communication principles and strategies, businesses can improve collaboration, enhance productivity, build stronger relationships, resolve conflicts, and increase customer satisfaction. Effective communication is a vital tool for success in the business world, and embracing this rule will ultimately lead to improved overall business performance.

Chapter 53: The Law of Customer Satisfaction

Customer satisfaction is a crucial factor in business success. The Law of Customer Satisfaction emphasizes the importance of meeting and exceeding customer expectations to build strong relationships, foster loyalty, and drive repeat business. Satisfied customers are more likely to become brand advocates, recommend the business to others, and continue to support it.

Understanding Customer Satisfaction:

Customer satisfaction refers to the evaluation of a customer's experience with a product or service based on their expectations. When customers are satisfied, they perceive that their needs have been met or exceeded, resulting in a positive overall experience. On the other hand, unsatisfied customers can lead to negative word-of-mouth, decreased customer loyalty, and potentially lost business.

Key Principles of Customer Satisfaction:

1. *Consistently deliver on promises:* Meeting or exceeding customer expectations is crucial for building trust and satisfaction. Making promises that cannot be fulfilled can lead to dissatisfaction and loss of credibility.

2. *Provide exceptional customer service:* Customers value excellent service. Responding promptly to inquiries, being attentive and friendly, and resolving issues effectively are key components of outstanding customer service.

3. *Personalize the customer experience:* Tailoring the experience to individual customer preferences and needs enhances satisfaction. By understanding their preferences and anticipating their needs, businesses can provide unique and personalized experiences.

4. *Seek and act on customer feedback:* Actively soliciting feedback from customers and taking actions to address their concerns or suggestions shows that the business values their opinions. This can lead to increased satisfaction and loyalty.

Strategies for Maximizing Customer Satisfaction:

1. *Create a customer-centric culture:* Make customer satisfaction a top priority throughout the organization. Train employees to prioritize customer needs and provide exceptional service.

2. *Set clear customer service standards:* Establish clear expectations for customer service and communicate them to all employees. Provide guidelines for responding to customer inquiries and resolving issues.

3. *Measure customer satisfaction:* Use surveys, feedback forms, and other measurement tools to gather information about customer satisfaction levels. Regularly review and analyze the data to identify areas for improvement.

4. *Act on customer feedback:* Take immediate action on customer feedback to address any issues or areas for improvement. This demonstrates that customer satisfaction is taken seriously and shows a commitment to continuous improvement.

5. *Empower employees:* Give employees the authority to make decisions and resolve customer issues on their own. This enables them to provide timely and effective solutions, which can lead to increased customer satisfaction.

6. *Provide ongoing training:* Continuously train employees on customer service skills and techniques. Keep them up to date with the latest industry trends and best practices.

7. *Reward and recognize outstanding customer service:* Acknowledge and reward employees who consistently deliver exceptional customer service. This reinforces the importance of customer satisfaction and encourages a customer-centric mindset.

Conclusion:

The Law of Customer Satisfaction highlights the significance of meeting and exceeding customer expectations. By prioritizing customer satisfaction and implementing strategies to enhance the customer experience, businesses can build strong relationships, foster loyalty, and drive long-term success.

Chapter 54: The Rule of Business Relationships

In the fast-paced and interconnected world of business, building and nurturing strong relationships is crucial for success. The Rule of Business Relationships emphasizes the importance of cultivating positive connections with various stakeholders, including customers, suppliers, partners, and employees. These relationships provide a solid foundation for collaboration, trust, and mutual growth.

THE POWER OF BUSINESS RELATIONSHIPS

Business relationships are built on trust, respect, and open communication. They go beyond transactional interactions and focus on long-term connections that benefit all parties involved. The power of strong business relationships lies in: 1. Trust and Credibility: Building trust is essential for maintaining long-term relationships. When stakeholders trust your business, they are more likely to support you, recommend your products or services, and continue doing business with you. Trust is earned through consistent delivery of high-quality products or services, transparency, and reliable communication. 2. Collaboration and Partnership: Strong business relationships foster collaboration and partnership opportunities. By working with other businesses or stakeholders, you can combine resources, knowledge, and expertise to create innovative solutions and reach new markets. Collaboration leads to mutual growth and shared success. 3. Support and Advocacy: When you have strong relationships with customers, suppliers, and partners, they become advocates for your business. They help spread positive word-of-mouth, provide referrals, and vouch for the quality and reliability of your offerings. These endorsements can significantly impact brand reputation and attract new customers. 4. Market Insights and Opportunities: Building relationships with customers and industry peers ensures access to valuable market insights and emerging opportunities. By staying connected with your network, you can stay informed about market trends, customer preferences, and industry developments. This knowledge allows you to make informed business decisions and stay ahead of the competition.

STRATEGIES FOR BUILDING STRONG BUSINESS RELATIONSHIPS

Building strong business relationships requires time, effort, and a genuine desire to connect with others. Here are some strategies to cultivate and maintain strong business relationships: 1. Communication: Effective communication is the foundation of any relationship. Be responsive, listen actively, and engage in open and honest dialogue. Regularly check in with your stakeholders to understand their needs, address concerns, and provide updates. Clear and transparent communication builds trust and ensures that everyone is on the same page. 2. Personalization: Treat each stakeholder as an individual and tailor your interactions accordingly. Show genuine interest in their needs, preferences, and goals. By personalizing your approach, you demonstrate that you value their unique perspective and are committed to meeting their specific needs. 3. Mutual Value Creation: Focus on creating value for your stakeholders. Understand their pain points and offer solutions that address their challenges. Look for opportunities to collaborate and create win-win situations. When both parties benefit from the relationship, it strengthens the bond and fosters long-term loyalty. 4. Follow-Up and Follow-Through: Consistency is key in building strong relationships. Follow up on your commitments and deliver on your promises. Be reliable and trustworthy. By demonstrating your accountability and reliability, you build credibility and reinforce the trust in your business. 5. Continuous Relationship Management: Building relationships is an ongoing process. Regularly engage with your stakeholders, even when you are not actively pursuing business opportunities. Stay connected through email updates, newsletters, social media interactions, or face-to-face meetings. By consistently nurturing your relationships, you stay top of mind and maintain the connection. 6. Show Appreciation: Expressing gratitude and appreciation goes a long way in relationship building. Recognize the contributions and support of your stakeholders and show them that you value their partnership. Small gestures of appreciation, such as thank-you notes or exclusive discounts, can strengthen the bond and foster loyalty.

CONCLUSION

The Rule of Business Relationships underscores the importance of building and maintaining strong connections with customers, suppliers, partners, and employees. These relationships form the backbone of your business and contribute to its long-term success. By investing time, effort, and authenticity into cultivating these relationships, you can tap into their power, unlock new opportunities, and create a network of loyal advocates. Remember, successful businesses are built on strong relationships.

Chapter 55: The Law of Innovation Management

Innovation is a fundamental aspect of business that drives growth, increases competitiveness, and ensures long-term success in today's dynamic and rapidly changing marketplace. The Law of Innovation Management emphasizes the importance of effectively managing innovation within an organization to harness its full potential and drive meaningful outcomes.

THE ROLE OF INNOVATION MANAGEMENT

Innovation management refers to the systematic and strategic approach to managing innovation processes, resources, and activities within a business. It involves creating an environment that fosters creativity, encourages idea generation, and supports the development and implementation of innovative solutions. The Law of Innovation Management recognizes that innovation is not a one-time event, but an ongoing process that requires dedicated effort and attention. It stresses the need for businesses to proactively manage innovation to stay ahead of the competition, meet evolving customer needs, and seize new opportunities.

KEY PRINCIPLES OF INNOVATION MANAGEMENT

To effectively manage innovation, businesses must adhere to several key principles: 1.

Culture of Innovation:

Foster a culture that values and encourages innovation. Create an environment where employees feel empowered to experiment, take risks, and contribute their ideas. Encourage open communication and collaboration to cultivate a creative and innovative workforce. 2.

Resource Allocation:

Allocate resources, including time, funding, and talent, to support innovation initiatives. Establish dedicated teams or departments responsible for driving innovation and provide them with the necessary resources and autonomy to execute innovation projects. 3.

Clear Innovation Strategy:

Develop a clear innovation strategy aligned with the overall business objectives. Set specific goals, define target areas for innovation, and establish a roadmap to guide the innovation process. Identify the desired outcomes and metrics to measure the success of innovation efforts. 4.

Customer-Centric Approach:

Adopt a customer-centric approach to innovation by identifying customer needs, pain points, and preferences. Conduct market research, gather customer feedback, and involve customers in the innovation process. Leverage customer insights to guide the development and refinement of innovative solutions. 5.

Collaboration and Partnerships:

Foster collaboration both internally and externally. Encourage cross-functional teams to work together, share ideas, and leverage diverse perspectives. Seek collaborations and partnerships with external stakeholders, such as research institutions, startups, or industry experts, to access new knowledge, technologies, and resources. 6.

Continuous Learning and Improvement:

Embrace a mindset of continuous learning and improvement. Encourage employees to continually upgrade their skills, stay updated on industry trends, and seek out new knowledge. Regularly evaluate and review innovation processes and outcomes to identify areas for improvement and implement necessary adjustments. 7.

Risk Management:

Recognize that innovation inherently involves risks. Develop risk management strategies to identify, assess, and mitigate risks associated with innovation initiatives. Create a supportive environment where failures are seen as learning opportunities and encourage calculated risk-taking.

STRATEGIES FOR EFFECTIVE INNOVATION MANAGEMENT

To effectively manage innovation within a business, consider the following strategies: 1.

Establish an Innovation Framework:

Create a structured framework or process for managing innovation within the organization. This framework should outline the stages of the innovation process, the roles and responsibilities of team members, and the criteria for evaluating and prioritizing ideas. 2.

Encourage Idea Generation:

Foster a culture of idea generation by providing platforms and opportunities for employees to contribute their ideas. Implement mechanisms such as brainstorming sessions, idea challenges, and suggestion boxes to encourage and collect ideas from employees at all levels of the organization. 3.

Implement Idea Evaluation and Selection:

Establish criteria and a systematic process for evaluating and selecting ideas for further development. Consider factors such as strategic alignment, feasibility, market potential, and resource requirements. Involve relevant stakeholders in the evaluation process to ensure diverse perspectives. 4.

Allocate Resources:

Allocate appropriate resources, including funding, time, and talent, to support innovation initiatives. Ensure that innovation projects have dedicated resources and are not overshadowed by day-to-day operations. Continuously monitor and adjust resource allocation based on project progress and strategic priorities. 5.

Promote Cross-Functional Collaboration:

Encourage collaboration and knowledge sharing across different departments and functions within the organization. Break down silos and create opportunities for employees from different backgrounds and expertise to collaborate on innovation projects. This interdisciplinary approach can spark creativity and lead to more impactful innovations. 6.

Manage Intellectual Property:

Protect and manage intellectual property resulting from innovation activities. Establish protocols for documenting and securing intellectual property rights. Ensure that employees understand the importance of confidentiality and adhere to patenting or licensing processes when applicable. 7.

Measure and Evaluate Innovation:

Develop metrics and indicators to measure the success of innovation initiatives. Monitor key performance indicators related to innovation, such as the number of new products or services launched, revenue generated from innovative offerings, customer satisfaction improvements, and employee engagement in innovation activities. Regularly evaluate innovation outcomes and use the insights gained to inform future innovation efforts.

CONCLUSION

The Law of Innovation Management underscores the importance of effectively managing innovation within a business. By adopting a strategic and systematic approach to innovation, businesses can cultivate a culture of creativity, drive meaningful outcomes, and stay ahead of the competition. Through the application of key principles and strategies for innovation management, businesses can unlock their full innovative potential and achieve sustainable growth and success.

Chapter 56: The Rule of Resource Allocation

Resource allocation is a critical aspect of running a successful business. The Rule of Resource Allocation emphasizes the need to effectively allocate resources to achieve maximum efficiency and productivity. Every business has limited resources such as time, money, manpower, and technology. It is essential to allocate these resources strategically to optimize performance and achieve desired outcomes.

THE IMPORTANCE OF RESOURCE ALLOCATION

Resource allocation plays a vital role in determining the success or failure of a business. Efficient resource allocation ensures that the right resources are allocated to the right tasks and projects, maximizing output and minimizing waste. It allows businesses to make the most of their available resources, resulting in improved profitability, reduced costs, and increased competitiveness.

Key Principles of Resource Allocation

To effectively allocate resources, businesses need to consider the following key principles: 1. Assess Priorities: Prioritizing tasks and projects is crucial for resource allocation. Identify the most important activities that align with the company's strategic objectives and allocate resources accordingly. This ensures that resources are focused on high-impact areas. 2. Consider Constraints: Recognize any resource limitations and constraints. This may include limitations in budget, manpower, or time. Understanding these constraints helps businesses make informed decisions about resource allocation and manage expectations. 3. Evaluate ROI: Analyze the potential return on investment for each task or project. Allocate resources to activities that offer the highest return or impact on the business. This requires assessing the potential benefits, risks, and costs associated with each project. 4. Flexibility and Adaptability: Resource allocation should be flexible and adaptable to changing circumstances. Business environments are dynamic, and priorities can shift. Being able to reallocate resources quickly and efficiently ensures that the business can respond effectively to new opportunities or challenges. 5. Collaboration and Communication: Effective resource allocation requires collaboration and communication between different teams or departments. This ensures that resources are allocated in a coordinated manner, promoting efficiency and avoiding duplication of efforts.

Strategies for Effective Resource Allocation

To optimize resource allocation, businesses can implement the following strategies: 1. Regular Evaluation: Continuously evaluate resource allocation to ensure its alignment with business goals and changing market conditions. Regularly assess the effectiveness and efficiency of resource allocation strategies, making adjustments as necessary. 2. Data-Driven Decisions: Utilize data and analytics to inform resource allocation decisions. Use historical data, market trends, customer insights, and performance metrics to identify areas of improvement and guide resource allocation strategies. 3. Automation and Technology: Leverage automation tools and technology to streamline resource allocation processes. Automated systems can help in tracking and managing resources, ensuring optimal utilization and reducing the risk of errors. 4. Cross-Functional Collaboration: Encourage collaboration and communication between different departments and teams. This promotes a holistic approach to resource allocation, ensuring that resources are distributed based on the overall business objectives and priorities. 5. Regular Training and Development: Invest in training and development programs to enhance employees' skills and knowledge. Well-trained employees are better equipped to make resource allocation decisions and contribute to the overall efficiency of the business.

Conclusion

The Rule of Resource Allocation highlights the importance of effectively allocating resources to optimize business performance and achieve desired outcomes. By prioritizing tasks, considering constraints, evaluating ROI, and fostering collaboration, businesses can make informed resource allocation decisions. Implementing strategies such as regular evaluation, data-driven decisions, automation, cross-functional collaboration, and employee training further enhance resource allocation practices. By following the Rule of Resource Allocation, businesses can maximize efficiency, reduce costs, and achieve long-term success.

Chapter 57: The Law of Adaptability

In today's rapidly changing business environment, adaptability is crucial for long-term success. The Law of Adaptability emphasizes the importance of businesses being flexible, responsive, and open to change. It recognizes that the ability to adapt to new opportunities, challenges, and market trends is essential for staying relevant, gaining a competitive edge, and achieving sustainable growth. Adaptability allows businesses to navigate uncertainties, disruptions, and unexpected shifts in the market. It requires a mindset of continuous learning, agility, and resilience. By embracing the Law of Adaptability, businesses can position themselves as dynamic and proactive entities that thrive in times of uncertainty. Here are key principles and strategies for applying the Law of Adaptability in business: 1. Embrace a Growth Mindset: Adopting a growth mindset enables individuals and organizations to see challenges as opportunities for learning and improvement. Embrace the belief that abilities and skills can be developed through dedication and hard work. 2. Stay Agile: Develop the ability to respond quickly and effectively to changing circumstances. This requires a proactive approach to identifying emerging trends, customer needs, and competitive threats. Regularly evaluate and adjust strategies and tactics to stay ahead. 3. Monitor Market Trends: Stay informed about industry trends, technological advancements, and changes in consumer behavior. Conduct market research and competitor analysis to identify new opportunities and emerging threats. Use this information to inform strategic decision-making. 4. Adopt a Customer-Centric Approach: Put the customer at the center of your business operations. Continuously gather feedback, listen to customer needs and preferences, and adapt your products, services, and marketing strategies accordingly. Anticipate and exceed customer expectations to maintain a competitive edge. 5. Promote Continuous Learning: Encourage a culture of continuous learning and professional development within your organization. Provide opportunities for employees to acquire new skills, stay updated on industry trends, and embrace innovation. Foster a learning environment that values curiosity, experimentation, and knowledge sharing. 6. Build a Diverse Team: Embrace diversity in your workforce to bring in different perspectives, experiences, and skills. A diverse team promotes creativity, innovation, and adaptability. Encourage collaboration and foster an inclusive work environment where ideas are freely shared and valued. 7. Collaborate with Partners: Seek strategic partnerships and collaborations with other organizations that share similar goals and values. Collaborating with partners can provide access to new resources, expertise, and markets. Seek mutually beneficial relationships that allow for knowledge-sharing and joint problem-solving. 8. Plan for Contingencies: Anticipate potential risks, disruptions, and challenges that may arise. Develop contingency plans to mitigate the impact, should these situations occur. By having alternative strategies in place, you can adapt quickly and minimize potential damage to your business. 9. Foster Effective Communication: Maintain open and transparent communication channels within your organization. Encourage employees to share ideas, insights, and concerns. Regularly communicate changes, updates, and the rationale behind strategic decisions to ensure alignment and understanding. 10. Monitor and Evaluate Adaptations: Continuously evaluate the effectiveness of your adaptations and their impact on business performance. Regularly measure and analyze key metrics to assess the success of your strategies. Use this feedback loop to make informed adjustments and refine your approach. By applying the Law of Adaptability, businesses can position themselves as agile, innovative, and resilient entities. They can better navigate changing market dynamics, identify new opportunities, and respond effectively to customer needs. Adaptability is not just a survival strategy; it is a fundamental principle for achieving long-term success in today's ever-changing business landscape. Embrace adaptability, embrace growth, and embrace the future.

Chapter 58: The Rule of Financial Analysis

Financial analysis is a crucial aspect of business management and decision-making. The Rule of Financial Analysis emphasizes the importance of analyzing financial data to gain insights into a company's performance, identify trends, and make informed decisions about the allocation of resources. Financial analysis involves assessing a company's financial health, profitability, liquidity, solvency, and efficiency. It provides valuable information to stakeholders, including investors, lenders, and managers, to evaluate the company's financial position and make predictions about its future performance. To effectively analyze financial data, businesses need to consider various financial ratios and indicators. These include: 1. Liquidity ratios: These ratios measure a company's ability to meet its short-term obligations. Examples include the current ratio and the quick ratio. 2. Profitability ratios: These ratios assess a company's ability to generate profit from its operations. Examples include the gross profit margin, net profit margin, and return on equity. 3. Solvency ratios: These ratios evaluate a company's long-term financial stability and ability to meet its long-term obligations. Examples include debt-to-equity ratio and interest coverage ratio. 4. Efficiency ratios: These ratios measure a company's ability to utilize its assets and resources efficiently to generate revenue. Examples include inventory turnover ratio and accounts receivable turnover ratio. By analyzing these ratios and indicators, businesses can identify areas of strength and weakness, assess the effectiveness of financial management strategies and investment decisions, and make adjustments to improve their financial performance. Financial analysis also involves comparing a company's performance to industry benchmarks and competitors. This benchmarking allows businesses to identify areas where they are outperforming or underperforming their competitors and make strategic changes accordingly. Furthermore, financial analysis plays a crucial role in strategic planning and forecasting. By analyzing historical financial data and trends, businesses can make more accurate predictions and projections about their future performance and make informed decisions about resource allocation, investments, and growth strategies. In conclusion, the Rule of Financial Analysis emphasizes the importance of analyzing financial data to evaluate a company's financial health, make informed decisions, and achieve long-term success. By conducting thorough financial analysis, businesses can gain valuable insights, identify areas for improvement, and make strategic decisions to optimize their financial performance.

Chapter 59: The Law of Entrepreneurship

Entrepreneurship is the driving force behind innovation, economic growth, and job creation. The Law of Entrepreneurship emphasizes the key principles and strategies that aspiring entrepreneurs should embrace to increase their chances of success.

EMBRACING RISK AND UNCERTAINTY

One of the fundamental aspects of entrepreneurship is embracing risk and uncertainty. Entrepreneurs understand that starting a business involves taking calculated risks and venturing into uncharted territories. They recognize that failure is a natural part of the entrepreneurial journey and that learning from failure is essential for growth.

IDENTIFYING OPPORTUNITIES AND GAPS IN THE MARKET

Successful entrepreneurs have a keen eye for identifying opportunities and gaps in the market. They possess a deep understanding of their target audience and are constantly researching and analyzing market trends, consumer needs, and industry dynamics. By identifying unmet needs and gaps in the market, entrepreneurs can develop innovative products, services, and business models to address these opportunities.

CREATING A UNIQUE VALUE PROPOSITION

A strong value proposition is crucial for entrepreneurial success. Entrepreneurs must clearly articulate the unique value they bring to the market and how their products or services differentiate from competitors. By creating a compelling value proposition, entrepreneurs can attract customers, investors, and strategic partners.

BUILDING A SOLID BUSINESS PLAN

A well-structured and comprehensive business plan is an essential tool for entrepreneurs. It outlines the vision, mission, goals, and strategies of the business. A business plan helps entrepreneurs communicate their ideas to stakeholders, secure funding, and guide the execution of their business strategies.

SECURING FUNDING AND MANAGING FINANCES

Entrepreneurs often face significant challenges in securing funding for their ventures. It is essential for entrepreneurs to have a clear understanding of their financial needs and develop a comprehensive funding strategy. This may involve seeking investment from angel investors, venture capitalists, or crowdfunding platforms. Entrepreneurs should also develop financial management skills to effectively allocate resources, track financial performance, and make informed financial decisions.

BUILDING STRONG NETWORKS AND PARTNERSHIPS

Networking and building strong relationships are crucial for entrepreneurs. Through networking, entrepreneurs can connect with mentors, potential investors, strategic partners, and like-minded individuals. By fostering relationships and collaborations, entrepreneurs can gain valuable insights, share resources, and expand their reach.

EMBRACING CONTINUOUS LEARNING AND ADAPTATION

Entrepreneurship is a journey of continuous learning and adaptation. Successful entrepreneurs embrace a growth mindset and are constantly seeking new knowledge and skills. They adapt their strategies based on market feedback, consumer behavior, and changing industry trends. By continuously learning and adapting, entrepreneurs can stay ahead of the curve and remain competitive in the market.

CONCLUSION

The Law of Entrepreneurship emphasizes the key principles and strategies that entrepreneurs should embrace on their journey to success. By embracing risk, identifying opportunities, creating unique value propositions, building solid business plans, securing funding, building networks, and continuously learning and adapting, entrepreneurs can increase their chances of building successful and sustainable businesses. Entrepreneurship requires passion, resilience, and dedication, but with the right mindset and strategies, entrepreneurs can make a lasting impact in their industries and create meaningful change.

Chapter 60: The Rule of Decision Analysis

In the business world, making informed and strategic decisions is crucial for success. The Rule of Decision Analysis emphasizes the importance of evaluating multiple options and selecting the most favorable course of action based on a thorough analysis of potential outcomes, risks, and benefits. Effective decision analysis involves a systematic approach that helps business owners and leaders make decisions with confidence and clarity. By following the principles of decision analysis, businesses can optimize their decision-making process and improve overall outcomes. The first step in decision analysis is to define clear objectives. It is essential to have a clear understanding of what you want to achieve and what factors will contribute to the desired outcomes. Defining clear objectives helps in setting the direction and focus of the decision-making process. Next, gathering relevant information is key to making informed decisions. This involves collecting data, conducting research, and seeking input from stakeholders. By gathering information, you can have a comprehensive understanding of the situation, potential risks and benefits, and alternative options available. Once the information is gathered, evaluating potential outcomes becomes crucial. This involves assessing the benefits and drawbacks of each alternative and considering their potential impact on the business. Evaluating potential outcomes helps in identifying the best course of action that aligns with the defined objectives. Considering risks and uncertainties is another important aspect of decision analysis. Every decision comes with its own set of risks, and it is important to evaluate and quantify these risks. Understanding the potential risks involved allows for effective risk management and mitigation strategies. The next step in decision analysis is to apply decision-making tools and models. There are various tools and models available, such as decision trees, cost-benefit analysis, and SWOT analysis, that can assist in evaluating different alternatives and quantifying their potential outcomes. It is also crucial to involve stakeholders in the decision-making process. This can include seeking input from team members, experts, and other relevant parties. By involving stakeholders, you can gain different perspectives and ensure that the decision aligns with the needs and expectations of all parties involved. Finally, communicating the decision effectively is essential for successful implementation. Clear and concise communication ensures that all stakeholders understand the decision and their roles in executing it. Communicating the decision also helps in managing expectations and ensuring transparency throughout the process. By following the Rule of Decision Analysis and applying these strategies, businesses can optimize their decision-making process, increase efficiency, and achieve better outcomes. Decision analysis provides a structured framework for making informed and strategic decisions, leading to long-term success and growth in the business. In conclusion, the Rule of Decision Analysis emphasizes the importance of making informed and strategic decisions in the business world. By defining clear objectives, gathering relevant information, evaluating potential outcomes, considering risks and uncertainties, applying decision-making tools and models, involving stakeholders, and communicating the decision effectively, businesses can optimize their decision-making process and achieve better outcomes. Decision analysis is a valuable tool for business owners and leaders in navigating complex situations, managing risks, and driving success in a competitive marketplace.

Chapter 61: The Law of Leadership Development

In the fast-paced and ever-changing business landscape, effective leadership is crucial for success. The Rule of Leadership emphasizes the importance of continuous development and growth as a leader. Leadership development involves honing essential skills and qualities that inspire and guide others towards a common objective. Successful leaders possess certain characteristics and follow specific principles that set them apart. One of the key qualities of a great leader is being visionary. Visionary leaders have a clear picture of where they want to take their organization and can rally their team around a shared goal. They are able to communicate their vision effectively and inspire others to work towards its realization. Good communication skills are also a vital component of effective leadership. Leaders must be able to articulate their ideas clearly and listen actively to their team members. They create an environment where open and honest communication is encouraged, fostering trust and collaboration. Integrity is another crucial quality of a great leader. Leaders with integrity act ethically and honestly in all their interactions. They lead by example and hold themselves to the same high standards they expect from their team members. This creates a culture of trust and respect within the organization. Emotional intelligence is another important aspect of leadership development. Leaders with high emotional intelligence are able to understand and manage their own emotions, as well as effectively navigate the emotions of others. This enables them to build strong relationships, resolve conflicts, and motivate their team. Adaptability is also a key quality for leaders to possess. In today's rapidly changing business environment, leaders must be able to adapt to new circumstances and navigate through uncertainty. They are open to new ideas and perspectives, and are willing to modify their approach when necessary. Empowerment is a principle that leaders should embrace. Successful leaders believe in the potential of their team members and provide them with the resources and autonomy they need to succeed. They delegate tasks, offer opportunities for growth and development, and recognize and reward their team's achievements. Continuous learning and growth are essential for leadership development. Great leaders understand that they must constantly expand their knowledge and skills in order to effectively lead in a dynamic business environment. They seek opportunities for personal and professional development and encourage a culture of learning within their organization. By following the Law of Leadership Development and focusing on these qualities and principles, aspiring leaders can enhance their effectiveness and inspire their team members to achieve their full potential. Leadership development is an ongoing journey that requires commitment and dedication, but the rewards are well worth it.

Chapter 62: The Rule of Customer Relationship Management

In today's highly competitive business landscape, maintaining strong relationships with customers is vital for success. The Rule of Customer Relationship Management (CRM) emphasizes the importance of building and nurturing these relationships to drive customer loyalty, satisfaction, and ultimately, business growth. Customer Relationship Management involves a strategic approach to managing and enhancing interactions with customers throughout their journey with a business. It encompasses understanding customer needs, providing personalized experiences, and fostering long-term relationships. By applying the Rule of Customer Relationship Management, businesses can effectively engage with customers, address their concerns, and exceed their expectations. One key aspect of the Rule of Customer Relationship Management is the collection and analysis of customer data. By leveraging data analytics tools and technologies, businesses can gain valuable insights into customer preferences, behaviors, and purchasing patterns. This data-driven approach allows companies to tailor their marketing strategies, develop targeted campaigns, and personalize their offerings to meet individual customer needs. Strategies for implementing the Rule of Customer Relationship Management include:

1. DEVELOP A CUSTOMER-CENTRIC CULTURE

To effectively manage customer relationships, businesses must place the customer at the center of their operations. This involves instilling a customer-centric mindset across all levels of the organization. Employees should be trained to understand the importance of customer satisfaction and empowered to make decisions that prioritize customer needs.

2. IMPLEMENT A CRM SYSTEM

Investing in a robust CRM system can streamline customer interactions and improve overall efficiency. A CRM system enables businesses to centralize customer data, track customer interactions, and automate processes. By having a comprehensive view of customer information, businesses can better understand customer preferences, anticipate their needs, and provide a personalized experience.

3. FOSTER PROACTIVE CUSTOMER SUPPORT

Prompt and effective customer support is essential for building lasting relationships. Businesses should strive to provide proactive support by anticipating customer needs and addressing concerns before they arise. This can be achieved through effective communication channels, timely responses, and personalized assistance.

4. REGULARLY ENGAGE WITH CUSTOMERS

Regular engagement is crucial for maintaining strong relationships with customers. Businesses should utilize various channels such as email newsletters, social media, or loyalty programs to stay connected. By providing relevant and valuable content, businesses can keep customers informed, engaged, and loyal.

5. SEEK AND ACT ON CUSTOMER FEEDBACK

Listening to customer feedback is key to continuous improvement. Businesses should actively seek feedback through surveys, reviews, and customer satisfaction metrics. Analyzing this feedback and taking action demonstrates a commitment to customer satisfaction and allows businesses to address any issues promptly.

6. PERSONALIZE CUSTOMER INTERACTIONS

Treating customers as individuals and providing personalized experiences strengthens the connection between businesses and their customers. This can be achieved by tailoring marketing messages, offering personalized recommendations, and remembering customer preferences. Personalization shows customers that they are valued and understood.

7. BUILD LONG-TERM RELATIONSHIPS

Customer loyalty is built through sustained efforts to build long-term relationships. Businesses should prioritize customer retention by offering exclusive incentives, rewards, or loyalty programs. By focusing on building loyalty, businesses can benefit from repeat business, positive word-of-mouth, and increased customer lifetime value. By applying the Rule of Customer Relationship Management, businesses can cultivate strong customer relationships, drive customer loyalty, and increase business growth. Businesses that prioritize customer relationship management are better positioned to provide exceptional customer experiences and achieve long-term success.

Chapter 63: The Law of Goal Setting

Setting goals is a fundamental aspect of achieving success in both personal and business endeavors. The Law of Goal Setting emphasizes the importance of setting clear, specific, and measurable goals to drive motivation, focus, and achievement.

THE POWER OF GOAL SETTING

Goal setting is a powerful tool that provides direction and purpose to individuals and businesses alike. By setting goals, you create a roadmap that guides your actions and decisions, ensuring that you stay on track and work towards meaningful outcomes. Here are some key benefits of goal setting: 1. **Motivation:** Setting goals fuels motivation by giving you something meaningful to strive for. Goals provide a sense of purpose and excitement, driving you to take action and overcome challenges. 2. **Focus:** Goals provide clarity and help you prioritize tasks and activities that align with your objectives. They prevent you from getting distracted by unimportant or irrelevant tasks, allowing you to focus your time and energy on what truly matters. 3. **Measurement:** When goals are specific and measurable, you can track your progress and determine whether you're moving in the right direction. Regularly assessing your progress helps you identify areas for improvement and make necessary adjustments. 4. **Accountability:** Setting goals creates a sense of accountability. By sharing your goals with others or having an accountability partner, you increase your commitment to achieving them and stay motivated throughout the journey. 5. **Time and resource management:** Goals provide a framework for effective time and resource management. When you have clear goals, you can allocate your time, energy, and resources in a way that supports their achievement, leading to increased productivity and efficiency.

PRINCIPLES OF EFFECTIVE GOAL SETTING

While setting goals is essential, it's equally important to approach goal setting in a strategic and effective manner. Here are some principles to follow when setting goals: 1. **Specific:** Goals should be specific, clearly defining what you want to achieve. Vague goals make it difficult to assess progress or create a plan of action. Instead of setting a goal to "increase sales," specify a numerical target like "increase sales revenue by 20% in the next quarter." 2. **Measurable:** Goals should be measurable, allowing you to track progress and determine whether you're moving closer to your desired outcome. Measurable goals have clear criteria for success, such as a specific number, percentage, or deadline. 3. **Achievable:** Goals should be challenging yet realistic. While it's important to set ambitious goals that stretch your capabilities, setting unattainable goals can lead to frustration and demotivation. Consider your resources, capabilities, and timeframes when setting goals. 4. **Relevant:** Goals should be aligned with your overall objectives and values. Your goals should contribute to your long-term vision and reflect what you truly desire to achieve. Aligning goals with your values ensures that you stay motivated and engaged throughout the process. 5. **Time-bound:** Goals should have a clear timeframe or deadline. A specific timeline creates a sense of urgency and helps you prioritize tasks. Setting deadlines also allows you to evaluate your progress and make any necessary adjustments along the way.

STRATEGIES FOR EFFECTIVE GOAL SETTING

To maximize the effectiveness of your goal-setting process, consider implementing the following strategies: 1. **Write it down:** Putting your goals in writing enhances clarity and commitment. Write down your goals in a specific and concise manner, and place them somewhere visible as a reminder of what you're working towards. 2. **Break it down:** Large goals can be overwhelming, so break them down into smaller, manageable steps. This makes the goals more attainable and allows you to track progress more effectively. 3. **Create an action plan:** Outline the actions and milestones needed to achieve your goals. Identify the specific steps, resources, and timelines required for each task. Having a clear plan makes it easier to stay organized and focused. 4. **Track your progress:** Regularly assess your progress towards your goals. This can be done through periodic check-ins or reviews, where you compare your actual progress against your plan. Use this feedback to stay motivated and make adjustments if necessary. 5. **Celebrate milestones:** Acknowledge and celebrate your achievements along the way. Recognizing milestones not only boosts morale but also provides a sense of accomplishment and motivation to keep pushing forward. 6. **Stay flexible:** Recognize that circumstances may change, and adjustments may be necessary. Be open to reviewing and modifying your goals when needed to ensure they remain relevant and aligned with your overall objectives.

CONCLUSION

The Law of Goal Setting emphasizes the importance of setting clear, specific, and measurable goals to drive motivation, focus, and achievement. By following the principles of effective goal setting and implementing strategic strategies, you can optimize your goal-setting process and increase your chances of successful outcomes. Remember, setting goals is not a one-time activity but an ongoing process that requires continuous evaluation, adjustment, and commitment.

Chapter 64: The Rule of Conflict Management

Conflict is an inevitable part of business and can arise from differences in opinions, goals, or expectations. However, effectively managing conflicts is crucial for maintaining harmonious relationships and achieving successful outcomes. The Rule of Conflict Management emphasizes the importance of addressing conflicts proactively and constructively.

THE ROLE OF CONFLICT MANAGEMENT

Conflict management refers to the strategies and techniques used to handle and resolve conflicts in a way that minimizes negative impacts and fosters positive outcomes. By managing conflicts effectively, businesses can prevent escalation, improve communication, enhance teamwork, and promote a healthier work environment.

The Negative Impact of Unresolved Conflict

When conflicts are left unresolved, they can have detrimental effects on both individuals and the overall organization. Unresolved conflict may lead to increased stress, decreased productivity, low morale, reduced collaboration, and even employee turnover. Furthermore, unresolved conflict can create a toxic work environment and damage relationships with clients, partners, and stakeholders.

The Benefits of Conflict Management

Proactively managing conflicts brings numerous benefits to a business. By addressing conflicts in a timely and constructive manner, businesses can: 1. Preserve Relationships: Conflict management allows for open dialogue and a better understanding of different perspectives, leading to stronger and more positive relationships among team members. 2. Improve Communication: Effective conflict management encourages transparent and honest communication, enhancing understanding and problem-solving between individuals or teams. 3. Foster Innovation: Resolving conflicts can unlock creativity and new ideas that arise from diverse viewpoints, leading to innovative solutions and improvements in business processes. 4. Enhance Decision-Making: Conflict management encourages thorough discussions and the exploration of various perspectives, ultimately leading to better-informed decisions. 5. Increase Productivity: By resolving conflicts, businesses can minimize disruptions, reduce stress, and create a more harmonious work environment, resulting in increased productivity and efficiency.

STRATEGIES FOR CONFLICT MANAGEMENT

To effectively manage conflicts, it is important to employ strategies that promote open communication, understanding, and collaboration. Here are some key strategies for conflict management:

1. Define the Issue

Start by clearly defining the conflict and understanding the underlying causes. Identify the specific issues and interests involved, and separate them from personal emotions or biases.

2. Foster Open Communication

Encourage individuals involved in the conflict to express their opinions, concerns, and feelings in a respectful and constructive manner. Active listening plays a vital role in understanding different perspectives and finding common ground.

3. Seek Common Ground

Look for areas of agreement or shared goals among the conflicting parties. Finding common ground can help in generating solutions that satisfy everyone's interests and lead to a win-win outcome.

4. Explore Different Solutions

Brainstorm various potential solutions by considering different perspectives and ideas. Encourage creative thinking and evaluate the feasibility and effectiveness of each proposed solution.

5. Mediation and Facilitation

In more complex or intense conflicts, it may be helpful to involve a neutral third party, such as a mediator or facilitator, to guide the process and facilitate open communication and understanding among the conflicting parties.

6. Emphasize Collaboration

Promote teamwork and collaboration among the conflicting parties to encourage a cooperative approach to problem-solving. Encourage individuals to work together towards a shared goal, focusing on finding mutually beneficial solutions.

7. Focus on the Future

While addressing past issues is important, ensure that the focus remains on finding solutions and moving forward. Encourage individuals to learn from the conflict and develop strategies to prevent similar issues in the future.

8. Learn and Improve

Conflict management should be viewed as a learning opportunity for individuals and the organization as a whole. Encourage individuals to reflect on the conflict and identify areas for personal growth and development.

CONCLUSION

Conflict management is a critical aspect of successful business operations. By addressing conflicts proactively and constructively, businesses can resolve issues, improve communication and teamwork, and foster a healthy and productive work environment. By following the Rule of Conflict Management and implementing the strategies discussed, businesses can transform conflicts into opportunities for growth and positive change.

Chapter 65: The Law of Performance Evaluation

Performance evaluation is an essential process in business that involves assessing the effectiveness and efficiency of employees. The Law of Performance Evaluation emphasizes the importance of evaluating performance to drive improvement and achieve business objectives. By providing feedback, setting clear expectations, and recognizing achievements, businesses can enhance productivity, foster employee development, and create a positive and engaged work environment.

WHY IS PERFORMANCE EVALUATION IMPORTANT?

Performance evaluation plays a crucial role in business management and decision-making. Here are some key reasons why performance evaluation is important: 1. **Assessing Employee Effectiveness:** Performance evaluations allow businesses to evaluate how well employees are performing their roles and responsibilities. It helps identify areas of strength and areas for improvement, enabling businesses to provide targeted feedback and support for employee development. 2. **Setting Clear Expectations:** Performance evaluations provide an opportunity to clarify expectations and align individual performance with organizational goals. By setting clear goals and objectives, businesses can ensure that employees understand what is expected of them and have a clear roadmap for success. 3. **Driving Employee**

Development: Performance evaluations foster employee growth and development by identifying areas where employees can improve their skills and competencies. It allows businesses to provide targeted training and development opportunities to enhance performance and career progression. 4. **Recognizing Achievements:** Performance evaluations provide a platform to recognize and reward exceptional performance. By acknowledging and celebrating achievements, businesses can motivate employees and reinforce positive behavior and outcomes. 5. **Identifying Training and Support Needs:** Performance evaluations can help identify areas where employees may need additional training or support. It allows businesses to address knowledge gaps and provide resources to help employees succeed in their roles. 6. **Improving Employee Engagement:** Regular performance evaluations contribute to a positive and engaged work environment. It provides employees with opportunities to share their perspectives, concerns, and ideas, fostering open communication and collaboration between employees and management.

STRATEGIES FOR EFFECTIVE PERFORMANCE EVALUATION

To ensure effective performance evaluations, businesses can follow these strategies: 1. **Establish Clear Evaluation Criteria:** Clearly define the criteria for evaluating performance, including both quantitative and qualitative metrics. This helps ensure a consistent and fair evaluation process. 2. **Regular Check-ins:** Implement regular check-ins throughout the year to provide ongoing feedback and keep employees informed about their performance. This allows for timely course correction and provides opportunities for improvement. 3. **Two-Way Communication:** Encourage open and honest communication during performance evaluations. Provide employees with the opportunity to share their perspectives, challenges, and aspirations. This fosters engagement and ownership in the evaluation process. 4. **Professional Development Plans:** Collaborate with employees to create professional development plans based on their goals and aspirations. This helps align individual development with organizational objectives and promotes continuous learning. 5. **Consistent and Fair Evaluations:** Ensure evaluations are conducted consistently and fairly across all employees. Avoid biases and favoritism by using objective criteria and standardized evaluation processes. 6. **Recognize and Reward High Performers:** Acknowledge and reward exceptional performance to motivate employees and reinforce positive behavior. This can include monetary rewards, promotions, or special recognition programs. 7. **Constructive Feedback:** Provide constructive feedback that focuses on areas for improvement and growth. Be specific and provide actionable recommendations to help employees develop their skills. 8. **Follow-Up and Accountability:** Establish a follow-up process to monitor progress on action items discussed during the performance evaluation. Hold both employees and managers accountable for their commitments.

CONCLUSION

The Law of Performance Evaluation highlights the importance of evaluating employee performance to drive improvement and achieve business objectives. By providing feedback, setting clear expectations, recognizing achievements, and promoting employee development, businesses can enhance productivity, foster a positive work environment, and align individual performance with organizational goals. Effective performance evaluations contribute to employee engagement, talent retention, and overall business success.

Chapter 66: The Rule of Talent Acquisition

Talent acquisition is a critical aspect of building a successful business. The Rule of Talent Acquisition emphasizes the importance of attracting and selecting top talent to drive business growth and achieve organizational objectives. Having a strong and effective talent acquisition strategy can give businesses a competitive advantage in the marketplace.

WHY IS TALENT ACQUISITION IMPORTANT?

Talent acquisition plays a crucial role in the success of a business. Here are some reasons why talent acquisition should be a priority: 1.

Access to top talent:

Effective talent acquisition allows businesses to attract and hire individuals who possess the skills, experience, and expertise required to excel in their respective roles. Having top talent onboard ensures that the business can meet its objectives and stay ahead of the competition. 2.

Enhanced performance and productivity:

Hiring the right talent leads to increased performance and productivity within the organization. When employees are well-matched to their roles and have the necessary skills and capabilities, they can perform their tasks more efficiently and effectively, resulting in improved business outcomes. 3.

Innovation and creativity:

Hiring talented individuals with diverse backgrounds and perspectives can bring fresh ideas and innovative thinking to the organization. This diversity of thought fosters a culture of creativity and innovation, driving business growth and helping companies stay ahead in a rapidly evolving business landscape. 4.

Employee retention:

Talent acquisition is not just about attracting top talent; it is also about retaining them. By selecting candidates who align with the company's values, goals, and culture, businesses can improve employee satisfaction and reduce turnover. This, in turn, leads to cost savings associated with recruitment, onboarding, and training. 5.

Building a strong employer brand:

A well-executed talent acquisition strategy contributes to building a strong employer brand. When businesses are known for their ability to attract and retain top talent, they become more attractive to prospective employees. A positive employer brand can help businesses attract a pool of high-quality candidates, enabling them to select the best fit for their organization.

STRATEGIES FOR EFFECTIVE TALENT ACQUISITION

To ensure the success of your talent acquisition efforts, it is important to implement effective strategies. Here are some key strategies to consider: 1.

Defining job requirements and criteria:

Before initiating the recruitment process, it is essential to clearly define the job requirements, qualifications, and criteria for each role. This helps in attracting candidates who possess the necessary skills and experience. 2.

Utilizing multiple sourcing channels:

To reach a diverse pool of candidates, it is important to utilize multiple sourcing channels such as online job boards, social media platforms, professional networks, and referrals. This increases the likelihood of finding highly qualified candidates who may not be actively searching for job opportunities. 3.

Building a strong employer brand:

A strong employer brand helps attract top talent. It is important to proactively manage your employer brand through positive employee experiences, effective communication, and showcasing the company's mission, values, and culture. 4.

Streamlining the selection process:

A streamlined and efficient selection process is crucial for attracting and securing top talent. This includes defining the steps, conducting thorough interviews, assessing candidates' skills and cultural fit, and providing timely feedback throughout the process. 5.

Offering competitive compensation and benefits:

To attract and retain top talent, it is important to offer competitive compensation and benefits packages. This includes market-based salaries, performance-based incentives, and comprehensive health and wellness benefits. 6.

Investing in employee development:

Talent acquisition is not just about hiring; it is also about investing in the development of employees. Offering opportunities for growth, training, and career advancement helps attract high-potential candidates who are committed to personal and professional development. 7.

Measuring and evaluating recruitment outcomes:

It is important to continuously measure and evaluate the outcomes of your talent acquisition efforts. This includes analysis of recruitment metrics such as time-to-fill, cost per hire, and retention rates. These insights can inform future talent acquisition strategies and help improve the overall recruitment process.

CONCLUSION

The Rule of Talent Acquisition emphasizes the importance of attracting and selecting top talent to drive business success. By implementing effective talent acquisition strategies, businesses can access top talent, enhance performance and productivity, foster innovation, improve employee retention, and build a strong employer brand. Investing in talent acquisition is an investment in the long-term success and growth of the organization.

Chapter 67: The Law of Succession Planning

Succession planning is a crucial aspect of business management that ensures the smooth transition of leadership and the continuity of operations beyond the current leadership. It involves identifying and developing potential leaders who can step into key positions when needed. The Law of Succession Planning emphasizes the importance of effectively managing leadership succession to maintain business stability, foster growth, and achieve long-term success. Successful succession planning encompasses several key principles:

1. IDENTIFYING KEY POSITIONS:

The first step in succession planning is identifying key positions within the organization. These positions play a critical role in driving business strategy and achieving organizational objectives. By identifying these positions, businesses can focus their efforts on developing the necessary skills and competencies in potential successors.

2. ASSESSING LEADERSHIP COMPETENCIES:

To ensure effective succession planning, it is essential to assess the leadership competencies required for each key position. This involves identifying the specific skills, knowledge, and experience necessary for success in these roles. By assessing leadership competencies, businesses can identify gaps and develop targeted development programs to bridge them.

3. DEVELOPING A TALENT PIPELINE:

Succession planning involves developing a talent pipeline of potential leaders who can fill key positions when they become vacant. This requires identifying high-potential employees within the organization and providing them with the necessary training, development, and mentoring opportunities to prepare them for future leadership roles. By developing a talent pipeline, businesses can ensure a pool of capable leaders ready to step into critical positions.

4. BUILDING LEADERSHIP CAPABILITIES:

Effective succession planning involves actively building leadership capabilities within the organization. This includes providing leadership development programs, coaching, and mentoring opportunities to potential successors. By investing in their growth and development, businesses can enhance their leadership capabilities and readiness for future roles.

5. CREATING A SUCCESSION PLAN:

A succession plan outlines the specific steps and timeline for transitioning leadership positions. It includes identifying potential successors, outlining their development plans, and determining the criteria and process for selecting the right candidate to fill each key position. The succession plan should be documented and communicated to all stakeholders to ensure a smooth and transparent transition.

6. COMMUNICATING THE SUCCESSION PLAN:

Communication is a crucial aspect of successful succession planning. Business leaders should communicate the succession plan to all relevant stakeholders, including employees, shareholders, and external partners. Clear communication helps build trust, manage expectations, and ensure a smooth transition of leadership. It also allows potential successors to understand their role and responsibilities in advance, facilitating their preparation for future leadership positions. Implementing effective strategies for succession planning brings several benefits to businesses: - Continuity and Stability: Succession planning ensures that there is a clear strategy in place for the continuation of business operations in the event of leadership changes. This provides stability and minimizes disruptions, allowing the business to maintain its momentum and thrive. - Reduced Risks: Succession planning helps businesses mitigate risks associated with leadership changes, such as a loss of key talent or a decline in performance during the transition period. By identifying and developing potential successors in advance, businesses can minimize these risks and ensure a seamless transition. - Talent Development: Succession planning creates a culture of talent development and growth within the organization. By investing in the development of potential successors, businesses can harness the full potential of their employees and foster a strong talent pipeline. - Improved Employee Engagement: Succession planning sends a positive message to employees that the organization is invested in their growth and development. This can boost employee morale, job satisfaction, and engagement, leading to higher productivity and retention rates. - Strategic Alignment: Succession planning allows businesses to align their leadership pipeline with their long-term strategic goals. By developing leaders who are aligned with the organization's values, vision, and objectives, businesses can ensure the effective execution of their strategic plans. In conclusion, the Law of Succession Planning highlights the importance of effectively managing leadership succession in businesses. By identifying key positions, assessing leadership competencies, developing a talent pipeline, building leadership capabilities, creating a succession plan, and communicating it effectively, businesses can ensure a smooth transition of leadership, maintain stability, and achieve long-term success. Successful succession planning contributes to continuity, talent development, risk management, and strategic alignment, enhancing the overall performance and growth of the business.

Chapter 68: The Rule of Competitive Intelligence

Competitive intelligence plays a vital role in the success and growth of a business. It involves gathering and analyzing information about competitors and their strategies to gain a competitive advantage in the market. The Rule of Competitive Intelligence emphasizes the importance of knowing your competition and using that knowledge to make informed business decisions. By understanding the competitive landscape, businesses can identify opportunities for innovation, anticipate market trends, and develop effective strategies to stay ahead.

WHY IS COMPETITIVE INTELLIGENCE IMPORTANT?

Competitive intelligence allows businesses to gain valuable insights into their competitors' strengths, weaknesses, and strategies. Here are some key reasons why competitive intelligence is important: 1. **Identifying your competitive advantage:** By analyzing competitors, businesses can determine their unique selling points and differentiate themselves in the market. This understanding helps in highlighting the value proposition that sets them apart from competitors. 2. **Anticipating market trends and customer preferences:** Competitor analysis helps businesses stay ahead of changes in the market and identify new trends and customer preferences. This allows them to adapt their products, services, and strategies accordingly. 3. **Identifying growth opportunities:** By studying competitors, businesses can uncover untapped market segments, identify potential partnerships or mergers, and develop new products or services to capitalize on emerging opportunities. 4. **Developing effective marketing and pricing strategies:** Competitive intelligence helps businesses understand how their competitors position themselves in the market and how they promote and price their products or services. This information allows businesses to develop effective marketing and pricing strategies that align with customer expectations and achieve a competitive edge. 5. **Reducing risks and making better decisions:** Understanding the competitive landscape helps businesses identify potential risks, such as new market entrants or competitive threats. This knowledge empowers businesses to make better-informed decisions and develop strategies to mitigate risks.

STRATEGIES FOR GATHERING COMPETITIVE INTELLIGENCE

To effectively gather competitive intelligence, businesses can employ various strategies. Here are some key methods: 1. **Market research:** Conducting market research allows businesses to gather data on industry trends, customer preferences, and competitor strategies. This can be done through surveys, focus groups, and analyzing industry reports and publications. 2. **Monitoring competitor websites and social media:** Regularly monitoring competitor websites, social media platforms, and online content can provide insights into their products, promotions, and customer interactions. This helps businesses stay updated on competitor activities. 3. **Attending industry events and conferences:** Participating in industry events and conferences provides opportunities to network with industry leaders, learn about industry trends, and gain insights into competitor strategies. 4. **Examining public information and financial reports:** Analyzing public information, such as annual reports, financial statements, and press releases, can provide valuable information about competitors' financial performance, growth plans, and business strategies. 5. **Engaging with industry experts and consultants:** Seeking guidance from industry experts and hiring consultants can provide businesses with expert insights and perspectives on competitor activities and industry trends.

APPLYING COMPETITIVE INTELLIGENCE IN BUSINESS

Once competitive intelligence is gathered, it is crucial to analyze the information and apply it strategically. Here are some key ways businesses can utilize competitive intelligence: 1. **Product and service development:** By analyzing competitors' products and services, businesses can identify gaps in the market and develop innovative offerings that meet customer needs. 2. **Pricing and promotions:** Competitive intelligence helps businesses determine optimal pricing strategies by understanding how competitors price their products and services. It also allows businesses to develop effective promotional campaigns to differentiate themselves and attract customers. 3. **Marketing and branding:** Analyzing competitor marketing strategies helps businesses position their brand effectively, target the right audience, and develop compelling marketing messages that differentiate them from competitors. 4. **Sales and customer acquisition:** By understanding how competitors target and acquire customers, businesses can develop effective sales strategies and customer acquisition techniques to gain a competitive edge. 5. **Market expansion and partnerships:** Competitive intelligence helps businesses identify new markets, potential partners, and areas for expansion. This knowledge allows businesses to enter new markets strategically and develop valuable partnerships. In conclusion, the Rule of Competitive Intelligence highlights the importance of understanding competitors and their strategies in order to gain a competitive advantage. By gathering and analyzing competitive intelligence, businesses can make informed decisions, anticipate market trends, and develop effective strategies that enhance their growth and success in the marketplace.

Chapter 69: The Law of Corporate Governance

Corporate governance is the system of rules, practices, and processes by which a company is directed and controlled. It encompasses the relationships between a company's management, board of directors, shareholders, and other stakeholders. The Law of Corporate Governance is essential for promoting transparency, accountability, and ethical behavior within organizations. It sets the standards for how companies should be managed and operated to ensure long-term success and protect the interests of shareholders and stakeholders.

PRINCIPLES OF CORPORATE GOVERNANCE

1. Transparency: Transparency refers to the disclosure of information that allows stakeholders to make informed decisions. Companies should provide accurate, timely, and comprehensive information about their financial performance, strategies, risks, and governance structure. 2. Accountability: Accountability ensures that individuals and entities responsible for corporate decisions and actions are held responsible for their behavior. This includes holding directors and executives accountable for their fiduciary duties, ensuring compliance with laws and

regulations, and promoting ethical behavior. 3. Fairness: Fairness emphasizes the equitable treatment of all stakeholders, including shareholders, employees, customers, suppliers, and the community. It involves treating all stakeholders with respect, ensuring equal opportunities, and avoiding conflicts of interest. 4. Independence: Independence promotes unbiased decision-making and objective oversight. This includes having independent directors on the board who can provide impartial judgment and challenge management decisions when necessary. 5. Responsibility: Responsibility refers to the obligation of companies to consider the impact of their actions on society and the environment. It involves corporate social responsibility, environmental stewardship, and sustainable practices that contribute to the well-being of society.

KEY ELEMENTS OF CORPORATE GOVERNANCE

1. Board of Directors: The board of directors is responsible for overseeing the strategic direction, risk management, and corporate performance of the company. It is composed of a diverse group of independent directors who bring different perspectives and expertise to the decision-making process. 2. Shareholder Rights: Shareholders have certain rights, such as the right to vote on important matters, the right to receive relevant information, and the right to share in the company's profits. These rights should be protected and respected by the company. 3. Code of Ethics: Companies should establish a code of ethics that outlines the expected behavior and ethical standards for directors,

executives, and employees. This code should promote integrity, honesty, fairness, and respect for all stakeholders. 4. Risk Management: Effective risk management is crucial for minimizing potential risks and maximizing shareholder value. Companies should have a comprehensive risk management framework in place to identify, assess, and mitigate risks. 5. Internal Controls: Internal controls are mechanisms and processes designed to safeguard company assets, ensure accurate financial reporting, and promote compliance with laws and regulations. This includes segregation of duties, internal audits, and regular monitoring and reporting. 6. Compensation and Incentives: The compensation of directors, executives, and employees should be fair, transparent, and aligned with the long-term interests of the company and its shareholders. This includes designing performance-based incentives that promote accountability and discourage excessive risk-taking.

BENEFITS OF EFFECTIVE CORPORATE GOVERNANCE

1. Enhanced Performance: Effective corporate governance can lead to improved financial performance, increased profitability, and long-term growth. Companies with strong governance practices are more attractive to investors and have a greater chance of success in the market. 2. Investor Confidence: Transparent and accountable corporate governance practices build trust and confidence among investors. This can attract new investors, reduce the cost of capital, and increase shareholder value. 3. Risk Mitigation: Strong corporate

governance helps identify and mitigate risks, ensuring that the company is better equipped to navigate challenges and uncertainties. This reduces the potential for legal and reputational risks. 4. Stakeholder Trust: Corporate governance practices that prioritize fairness, transparency, and responsibility foster trust and loyalty among stakeholders. This enhances relationships with employees, customers, suppliers, and the community. 5. Long-Term Sustainability: Effective corporate governance provides a solid foundation for long-term sustainability. It ensures that the company operates ethically, complies with laws and regulations, and considers the environmental and social impact of its actions.

CONCLUSION

The Law of Corporate Governance is vital for promoting transparency, accountability, and ethical behavior within organizations. By adhering to the principles of corporate governance and implementing effective governance practices, companies can enhance performance, build investor confidence, mitigate risks, and foster trust among stakeholders. Good corporate governance is an essential component of long-term success and profitability in today's business landscape.

Chapter 70: The Rule of Strategic Partnerships

In today's dynamic and interconnected business landscape, strategic partnerships have become increasingly vital for success. The Rule of Strategic Partnerships emphasizes the significance of collaborating with other organizations to drive growth, enhance competitiveness, and achieve mutual goals. A strategic partnership refers to a formal alliance between two or more organizations that share resources, knowledge, expertise, and capabilities to create value and achieve strategic objectives. These partnerships can take various forms, such as joint ventures, alliances, mergers, acquisitions, and consortiums. The key is to establish a mutually beneficial relationship that leverages the strengths of each partner to gain a competitive advantage in the market. The Rule of Strategic Partnerships brings several benefits to businesses. First and foremost, it allows companies to access new markets, customers, and distribution channels that may otherwise be difficult to reach independently. By combining resources and networks, partners can penetrate new markets more efficiently and effectively. Additionally, strategic partnerships promote innovation and enable companies to leverage each other's expertise and knowledge. Collaborating with partners from different industries or backgrounds brings fresh perspectives and increases the likelihood of developing innovative solutions or products. This can lead to a competitive edge and differentiation in the market. Furthermore, strategic partnerships enable companies to mitigate risks and share the burden of costs and resources. By pooling resources and sharing risks, partners can undertake ambitious projects or ventures that would be more challenging or costly to pursue alone. This risk-sharing aspect of strategic partnerships reduces the downside potential and increases the upside potential for both parties involved. Strategic partnerships also provide access to complementary resources, capabilities, or technologies that may not be available internally. Through collaboration, companies can tap into each other's strengths and fill gaps in their own capabilities. This enables partners to deliver more comprehensive and value-added solutions to customers, further enhancing their competitive advantage. To establish successful strategic partnerships, businesses must follow certain key principles. First and foremost, there must be a clear alignment of goals and values between the partners. A shared vision and common objectives provide a solid foundation for collaboration. Secondly, open and transparent communication is critical throughout the partnership. Regular and honest communication helps build trust, resolve conflicts, and identify opportunities for growth. It is also important to establish clear governance structures, roles, and responsibilities to ensure accountability and efficiency in decision-making. Another important aspect of strategic partnerships is the development of mutually beneficial agreements or contracts. These agreements should outline the specific objectives, resources, responsibilities, and benefits for each partner. Clear expectations and a fair distribution of value are essential for long-term success and harmony in the partnership. Furthermore, it is crucial to continuously monitor and evaluate the performance of the partnership. Regular assessments ensure that the partnership is meeting its intended goals and provides an opportunity to identify areas for improvement or adjustment. Flexibility and adaptability are key to responding to changing market conditions or dynamics within the partnership. In conclusion, the Rule of Strategic Partnerships highlights the importance of collaboration and cooperation in today's business world. Through strategic partnerships, businesses can access new markets, enhance innovation, share costs and risks, and leverage complementary resources. By following key principles and establishing mutually beneficial relationships, companies can strengthen their competitive advantage, drive growth, and achieve long-term success.

Chapter 71: The Law of Work-Life Balance

Achieving a healthy work-life balance is crucial for overall well-being and long-term success in both personal and professional spheres. The Law of Work-Life Balance emphasizes the importance of maintaining harmony between work commitments and personal life. In today's fast-paced and competitive business environment, finding a balance between the demands of work and personal responsibilities can be challenging, but it is essential for achieving a fulfilling and meaningful life.

THE IMPACT OF WORK-LIFE IMBALANCE

When work takes precedence over personal life, it can lead to detrimental effects on various aspects of an individual's well-being: 1. Health and Well-being: Neglecting personal needs and neglecting self-care can result in increased stress levels, burnout, and physical and mental health issues. Chronic stress can have long-term consequences on overall health and productivity. 2. Relationships: Work-life imbalance can strain relationships with family, friends, and loved ones. Lack of quality time and attention can lead to feelings of neglect and dissatisfaction among loved ones, ultimately impacting the overall quality of relationships. 3.

Productivity and Performance: Continuous work without sufficient rest and leisure time can lead to decreased productivity, reduced concentration, and lower job satisfaction. Over time, this can hinder performance and creativity, leading to diminishing returns in the workplace. 4. Mental Well-being: Allowing work to dominate life can contribute to a distorted work identity, where one's self-worth becomes solely dependent on professional achievements. This can lead to a sense of emptiness and unfulfillment in other areas of life.

STRATEGIES FOR ACHIEVING WORK-LIFE BALANCE

To maintain a healthy work-life balance, it is essential to adopt strategies that prioritize personal well-being and allow for meaningful engagement in both work and personal life. Here are some effective strategies to achieve work-life balance: 1. Set Priorities: Define personal and professional priorities to allocate time and energy appropriately. Identify and focus on activities that align with personal values and long-term goals. 2. Establish Boundaries: Separate work and personal life by setting clear boundaries. Create designated time slots for work-related activities and non-work activities, and strive to maintain these boundaries to ensure quality time for both. 3. Schedule Leisure and Downtime: Dedicate specific time to engage in favorite hobbies, spend time with loved ones, and recharge. Prioritize self-care activities, such as exercise, relaxation, and hobbies, to prevent burnout and replenish energy levels. 4. Delegate and Seek Support: Learn to delegate tasks and responsibilities whenever possible and rely on the support of colleagues, friends, and family. Delegate tasks that can be handled by others, enabling a more balanced distribution of work and responsibilities. 5. Practice Effective Time Management: Enhance productivity by practicing effective time management techniques such as prioritizing tasks, setting realistic deadlines, and avoiding multitasking. Utilize tools and technologies to streamline work processes and improve efficiency. 6. Practice Mindfulness and Stress Management: Incorporate mindfulness practices such as meditation, deep breathing exercises, and regular breaks throughout the day to manage stress levels. Take short breaks to disconnect from work and recharge. 7. Communicate Openly: Maintain open and honest communication with supervisors, colleagues, and family members about your priorities and boundaries. Advocate for your needs and seek understanding and support from those around you. 8. Embrace Flexibility: Explore flexible work arrangements such as telecommuting, flexible hours, or job sharing if feasible. Flexible work options can provide opportunities to balance personal and professional commitments effectively. 9. Be Present and Engaged: When dedicating time to work or personal activities, be fully present and engaged. Avoid distractions and focus on the task at hand. This allows for greater efficiency and enjoyment in each area of life. 10. Regularly Evaluate and Adjust: Regularly reassess your work-life balance and make necessary adjustments. Be flexible and adaptable, knowing that balance may look different at different stages of life. Continually reevaluate priorities and adjust routines accordingly.

BENEFITS OF WORK-LIFE BALANCE

Striving for a healthy work-life balance offers numerous benefits: 1. Enhanced Well-being: Achieving a work-life balance promotes overall well-being, leading to improved mental, physical, and emotional health. It reduces stress levels and increases happiness and life satisfaction. 2. Increased Productivity: Balancing work and personal life leads to increased productivity and efficiency. When individuals prioritize self-care and engage in non-work activities, they return to work refreshed and energized, positively impacting job performance. 3. Stronger Relationships: Maintaining a work-life balance allows for more quality time with loved ones, strengthening personal relationships. By prioritizing relationships, individuals experience stronger emotional connections and a deeper sense of fulfillment. 4. Job Satisfaction: Achieving work-life balance contributes to higher job satisfaction. It fosters a positive attitude towards work, improves engagement, and enhances overall job performance. 5. Retention and Attraction of Talent: Organizations that promote and support work-life balance have higher employee retention rates and are better positioned to attract top talent. Employees are more likely to stay with companies that value work-life balance and provide supportive policies. 6. Personal Growth and Fulfillment: Striking a balance between work and personal life allows individuals to engage in personal growth activities, explore interests, and pursue passions. It facilitates a sense of fulfillment and helps individuals lead well-rounded and meaningful lives.

CONCLUSION

Achieving a healthy work-life balance is crucial for overall well-being and long-term success. By adopting strategies that prioritize personal well-being and allow for meaningful engagement in both work and personal life, individuals can experience increased productivity, enhanced relationships, improved job satisfaction, and a greater sense of fulfillment. Embracing the Law of Work-Life Balance creates harmony, reduces stress, and contributes to a higher quality of life.

Chapter 72: The Rule of Influencer Marketing

In today's digital age, influencer marketing has emerged as a powerful strategy for businesses to reach and connect with their target audience. The Rule of Influencer Marketing emphasizes the importance of leveraging influential individuals to promote products, services, or brand messages to a larger audience.

THE POWER OF INFLUENCER MARKETING

Influencer marketing capitalizes on the trust and credibility that influencers have built with their followers. These individuals, who could be bloggers, social media personalities, or industry experts, have established a loyal following who looks to them for advice, recommendations, and inspiration. By partnering with influencers, businesses can tap into their influence and leverage their reach to effectively promote their brand and offerings. When done right, influencer marketing can yield several benefits for businesses. It allows them to: 1. Expand reach: Influencers have a dedicated following that aligns with a specific niche or target market. Partnering with them enables businesses to tap into that audience and extend their reach to potential customers who may not have been aware of their brand or product. 2. Build trust and credibility: Influencers have already fostered trust and credibility with their followers. When they endorse a product or service, their audience views it as a genuine recommendation, which can significantly influence their purchasing decisions. 3. Drive brand awareness: Through influencer partnerships, businesses can increase brand visibility and generate buzz around their products or services. By leveraging the reach and engagement of influencers, they can effectively raise awareness among their target audience. 4. Increase engagement and conversions: Influencers have the power to drive engagement and generate conversions. Their followers are more likely to engage with content recommended by the influencer, whether it's liking, commenting, sharing, or even making a purchase.

STRATEGIES FOR EFFECTIVE INFLUENCER MARKETING

To successfully implement influencer marketing, businesses should consider the following strategies: 1. Identify the right influencers: It's crucial to identify influencers who align with your brand values, target audience, and goals. Look for influencers who have a strong following, engagement, and a genuine connection with their audience. 2. Establish mutually beneficial partnerships: Approach influencers with a value proposition that highlights how partnering with your brand can benefit both parties. Provide them with clear guidelines and expectations for the collaboration. 3. Create authentic and engaging content: Collaborate with influencers to develop content that resonates with their audience while staying true to your brand's messaging. Encourage them to highlight the unique aspects of your product or service in an authentic and creative way. 4. Track and measure results: Set key performance indicators (KPIs) to measure the success of your influencer marketing campaigns. Track metrics such as reach, engagement, conversions, and brand sentiment to evaluate the effectiveness of your partnerships. 5. Foster long-term relationships: Building long-term relationships with influencers can yield greater benefits. Engage with influencers beyond a single campaign and develop ongoing collaborations to maintain brand visibility and continuous promotion. 6. Stay compliant: Ensure that your influencer marketing campaigns comply with relevant advertising and disclosure regulations. Clearly communicate any sponsored content or partnerships to maintain transparency and trust with the audience.

CONCLUSION

The Rule of Influencer Marketing highlights the power of leveraging influential individuals to promote your brand. By partnering with the right influencers and creating engaging content, businesses can expand their reach, build trust, and drive conversions. Embracing influencer marketing as part of your marketing strategy can significantly impact your brand's visibility and success in today's digital landscape.

Chapter 73: The Law of Market Research

Market research plays a crucial role in business decision-making. The Law of Market Research emphasizes the importance of gathering and analyzing relevant data to gain insights into market dynamics, customer preferences, and industry trends. By conducting effective market research, businesses can make informed decisions, develop targeted marketing strategies, and stay ahead of the competition.

THE IMPORTANCE OF MARKET RESEARCH

Market research provides valuable information about the target market, allowing businesses to understand customer needs and preferences. By collecting data on consumer behavior, purchasing habits, and demographic information, businesses can identify market trends, assess demand for products or services, and tailor their offerings to meet customer expectations. Market research also helps businesses identify opportunities for growth, analyze competitor strategies, and make informed investment decisions.

TYPES OF MARKET RESEARCH

There are two main types of market research: primary research and secondary research. Primary research involves collecting data directly from the target market through surveys, interviews, focus groups, and observations. This type of research provides firsthand information and allows businesses to gather specific insights tailored to their unique needs. Primary research is particularly useful for understanding customer preferences, testing new product concepts, and gathering feedback on existing offerings. Secondary research, on the other hand, involves gathering information from existing sources such as industry reports, government data, trade publications, and online resources. Secondary research provides a broader overview of the market and can be used to gather statistical data, analyze industry trends, and benchmark against competitors. It is a cost-effective method of obtaining information and can complement primary research findings.

THE MARKET RESEARCH PROCESS

The market research process typically involves the following steps: 1. Defining research objectives: Clearly articulate the goals and objectives of the research to guide the data collection and analysis process. 2. Designing the research methodology: Determine the most appropriate research methods and techniques to collect the necessary data. This may include surveys, interviews, focus groups, or a combination of methods. 3. Collecting data: Gather data from various sources, using the chosen research methods. Ensure the data collected is accurate, reliable, and representative of the target market. 4. Analyzing data: Use statistical tools and techniques to analyze the collected data and extract meaningful insights. Identify trends, patterns, and correlations that can inform business decisions. 5. Interpreting findings: Interpret the research findings in the context of the business objectives. Draw conclusions and make recommendations based on the analyzed data. 6. Implementing insights: Apply the insights gained from the market research to inform business strategies, marketing campaigns, product development, and other relevant areas. Use the findings to make data-driven decisions and optimize business performance.

BENEFITS OF MARKET RESEARCH

Market research provides several benefits for businesses, including: 1. Identifying opportunities: Market research helps uncover untapped market segments, emerging trends, and unmet customer needs, enabling businesses to develop new products or services and enter new markets. 2. Minimizing risks: By understanding customer preferences, market dynamics, and competitive landscapes, businesses can minimize risks associated with product launches, marketing campaigns, and investments. 3. Informing marketing strategies: Market research helps businesses develop targeted marketing strategies, identify the most effective communication channels, and craft messages that resonate with the target audience. 4. Improving customer satisfaction: By understanding customer preferences and expectations, businesses can tailor their offerings to meet customer needs, leading to higher levels of customer satisfaction and loyalty. 5. Enhancing competitiveness: Market research allows businesses to benchmark their performance against competitors, identify competitive advantages, and stay ahead of industry trends, leading to a stronger market position. 6. Driving innovation: Market research provides insights into emerging trends, customer preferences, and industry dynamics, helping businesses identify opportunities for innovation and strategic growth.

CONCLUSION

The Law of Market Research emphasizes the importance of gathering and analyzing relevant data to gain insights into market dynamics, customer preferences, and industry trends. Effective market research allows businesses to make informed decisions, develop targeted marketing strategies, and stay ahead of the competition. By investing in market research, businesses can identify opportunities, minimize risks, enhance customer satisfaction, improve competitiveness, and drive innovation.

Chapter 74: The Rule of Decision Making

In the world of business, decision making is a critical skill that can make or break the success of a venture. The Rule of Decision Making emphasizes the need for business owners to make informed and strategic decisions in order to steer their organizations towards growth and success. Effective decision making involves considering various factors, analyzing information, and choosing the best course of action. By following the principles of the Rule of Decision Making, business owners can optimize their decision-making process and achieve better outcomes.

CLEAR OBJECTIVES

One of the key principles of effective decision making is setting clear objectives. Before making any decision, it is crucial to define the desired outcome and understand what the decision aims to achieve. Setting clear objectives helps provide direction and focus, allowing business owners to make decisions that align with their overall goals and strategies. Without clear objectives, decision-making can become arbitrary and lack purpose.

GATHERING RELEVANT INFORMATION

Another important aspect of decision making is gathering relevant information. In order to make well-informed decisions, business owners need to collect and analyze pertinent data and insights. This may involve conducting market research, studying industry trends, reviewing financial reports, or seeking input from stakeholders. By gathering relevant information, business owners can gain a comprehensive understanding of the factors at play and make decisions based on solid evidence.

EVALUATING POTENTIAL OUTCOMES

One of the key steps in decision making is evaluating potential outcomes. This involves assessing the benefits and drawbacks of each possible decision and analyzing how they align with the defined objectives. By considering the potential consequences of different decisions, business owners can make choices that have a greater likelihood of achieving their desired outcomes. Evaluating potential outcomes requires critical thinking, weighing the pros and cons, and considering both short-term and long-term implications.

CONSIDERING RISKS AND UNCERTAINTIES

In addition to evaluating potential outcomes, effective decision making also involves considering risks and uncertainties. Every decision carries a level of risk, and business owners must assess the potential risks involved before making a final choice. By identifying and evaluating potential risks, business owners can implement strategies to mitigate or manage them effectively. This includes assessing the likelihood of risks occurring and the potential impact on the organization.

DECISION-MAKING TOOLS AND MODELS

To assist in the decision-making process, business owners can utilize various tools and models. Decision trees, cost-benefit analysis, SWOT analysis, and other frameworks can provide a systematic approach to analyzing options and evaluating their potential outcomes. These decision-making tools help structure the decision-making process, provide a framework for assessing alternatives, and facilitate objective analysis.

INVOLVING STAKEHOLDERS

The involvement of stakeholders is another important principle of effective decision making. Engaging stakeholders throughout the decision-making process helps ensure that multiple perspectives are considered and that decisions are well-informed and supported. Stakeholders may include employees, customers, investors, suppliers, and other key individuals or groups who can provide valuable insights and perspectives. Collaborating with stakeholders creates a sense of ownership and increases the likelihood of successful implementation.

COMMUNICATING DECISIONS EFFECTIVELY

Lastly, effective decision making involves communicating decisions clearly and effectively. Once a decision has been made, it is important to communicate the rationale behind it, the expected outcomes, and any action steps that need to be taken. Clear and timely communication allows all stakeholders to understand the decision and their roles in implementing it. Effective communication also fosters transparency, builds trust, and promotes a sense of alignment and unity. By following the principles and strategies of the Rule of Decision Making, business owners can optimize their decision-making process and achieve better outcomes. Clear objectives, gathering relevant information, evaluating potential outcomes, considering risks and uncertainties, utilizing decision-making tools and models, involving stakeholders, and communicating decisions effectively are all key elements of effective decision making. By making informed and strategic decisions, business owners can navigate challenges, seize opportunities, and steer their organizations towards growth and success.

Chapter 75: The Law of Financial Management

Financial management is a critical aspect of running a successful business. The Law of Financial Management emphasizes the importance of effectively managing finances to achieve long-term success and sustainability.

This chapter will delve into the key principles and strategies behind financial management, providing business owners with valuable insights and guidance.

THE IMPORTANCE OF FINANCIAL MANAGEMENT

Financial management plays a crucial role in business operations and decision-making. It involves the planning, organizing, controlling, and monitoring of financial resources to achieve the organization's goals and objectives. Here are some reasons why financial management is essential:

1. Financial Planning and Budgeting:

Effective financial management ensures that businesses have a clear financial plan and budget in place. This enables businesses to allocate resources efficiently, set realistic financial goals, and track progress towards those goals.

2. Resource Allocation:

Financial management helps businesses allocate their resources strategically. It involves analyzing the costs and benefits of different investment options and determining how to allocate funds to different departments or projects. By optimizing resource allocation, businesses can maximize their returns and minimize unnecessary expenses.

3. Risk Management:

Financial management involves assessing and managing financial risks. It helps businesses identify potential financial risks, such as fluctuations in the market, interest rate changes, or unexpected expenses, and develop strategies to mitigate these risks. By effectively managing risks, businesses can safeguard their financial stability and protect themselves from potential setbacks.

4. Profitability and Cash Flow:

Financial management involves monitoring and analyzing financial data to assess a business's profitability and cash flow. It helps businesses identify areas of profitability, manage costs, and ensure a steady cash flow to meet operational needs. This enables businesses to make informed decisions that positively impact their bottom line.

5. Financial Decision-Making:

Financial management provides businesses with the tools and information needed to make informed financial decisions. It helps businesses assess investment opportunities, evaluate financial alternatives, and analyze the potential impact of different decisions on their overall financial health. By making strategic financial decisions, businesses can optimize their financial performance and achieve their goals.

STRATEGIES FOR EFFECTIVE FINANCIAL MANAGEMENT

To effectively manage finances, businesses should adopt various strategies that align with the Law of Financial Management. Here are some key strategies to consider:

1. Develop a Financial Plan:

Create a comprehensive financial plan that outlines your business's short-term and long-term financial goals. This plan should include a budgeting process, revenue and expense forecasts, and financial performance indicators. Regularly review and adjust your financial plan based on changing market conditions and business needs.

2. Monitor Cash Flow:

Keep a close eye on your cash flow to ensure you have enough funds to cover operating expenses, pay creditors, and invest in growth opportunities. Implement cash flow management techniques such as invoicing promptly, monitoring accounts receivable, and controlling expenses to maintain a healthy cash flow.

3. Control Costs:

Regularly evaluate your business's expenses and identify areas where costs can be reduced or optimized. Look for opportunities to negotiate better deals with suppliers, streamline operations to eliminate unnecessary expenses, and implement cost-saving measures wherever possible.

4. Implement Internal Controls:

Establish strong internal controls to safeguard your business's financial assets and prevent fraud or financial mismanagement. This includes implementing proper segregation of duties, conducting regular internal audits, and implementing financial reporting systems to ensure accuracy and transparency.

5. Utilize Financial Technology:

Leverage financial technology (FinTech) tools and software to streamline financial processes, improve efficiency, and gain real-time insights into your business's financial health. Utilize accounting software, expense management systems, and financial analytics tools to simplify financial management tasks and make data-driven decisions.

6. Seek Professional Advice:

If you're not a financial expert, consider seeking professional advice from accountants, financial advisors, or consultants. These professionals can provide guidance on financial management best practices, help you interpret financial data, and offer strategic insights to improve your business's financial performance.

7. Continuously Monitor and Evaluate:

Regularly review and evaluate your business's financial performance against your financial plan and objectives. Analyze financial statements, key performance indicators, and trends to identify areas for improvement. Continuously monitor market conditions and adjust your financial strategies accordingly.

CONCLUSION

The Law of Financial Management emphasizes the importance of effectively managing finances to achieve long-term success in business. By implementing key financial management strategies and principles, businesses can optimize their financial health, make informed decisions, and achieve their financial goals. Remember to continually monitor and evaluate your financial performance to stay on track and adapt to changing market conditions.

Chapter 76: The Rule of Performance Management

Performance management is a crucial aspect of running a successful business. It involves setting clear expectations, monitoring employee performance, providing feedback and guidance, and recognizing and rewarding achievements. The Rule of Performance Management emphasizes the importance of effectively managing employee performance to drive overall organizational success. Effective performance management has numerous benefits for both the individual employee and the organization as a whole. It helps align individual goals and objectives with the broader organizational goals, enhances employee engagement and job satisfaction, identifies areas for improvement and development, and ultimately improves overall productivity and performance. To effectively apply the Rule of Performance Management, there are several key principles and strategies that businesses should consider: 1.

SET CLEAR EXPECTATIONS:

Clearly define performance expectations and goals for each employee, ensuring they are specific, measurable, achievable, relevant, and time-bound (SMART goals). Communicate these expectations clearly and transparently, ensuring employees understand what is expected of them. 2.

CONTINUOUS FEEDBACK:

Regularly provide feedback on employee performance, both positive and constructive. This feedback should be specific, timely, and actionable, focusing on behaviors and outcomes. Regular feedback helps employees stay on track, make improvements, and feel valued and supported. 3.

GOAL-SETTING AND DEVELOPMENT:

Help employees set personal and professional goals that align with their interests and career aspirations. Provide opportunities for skill development, training, and growth to help employees enhance their abilities and reach their full potential. 4.

PERFORMANCE REVIEWS:

Conduct regular performance reviews to assess employee performance against set goals and expectations. These reviews should be comprehensive, fair, and based on objective criteria. Use the reviews as a platform to provide feedback, discuss strengths and areas for improvement, and set new goals. 5.

REWARD AND RECOGNITION:

Recognize and reward exceptional performance to motivate and retain top-performing employees. This can be done through monetary rewards, promotions, bonuses, or non-monetary rewards such as public recognition or career development opportunities. 6.

SUPPORT AND COACHING:

Provide ongoing support and coaching to help employees overcome challenges and improve their performance. Offer guidance, resources, and training to address knowledge or skill gaps and create a supportive and nurturing environment. 7.

DOCUMENTATION AND RECORD-KEEPING:

Maintain accurate and up-to-date records of employee performance, including feedback, performance metrics, and any disciplinary actions or improvement plans. These records are essential for making informed decisions, tracking progress, and addressing performance issues. 8.

PERFORMANCE IMPROVEMENT PLANS:

Implement performance improvement plans when necessary to address persistent performance issues. These plans should outline specific steps and timelines for improvement, provide additional support and resources, and establish clear consequences if improvement is not achieved. 9.

FLEXIBILITY AND ADAPTABILITY:

Recognize that performance management strategies may need to be adjusted over time to meet changing business needs and individual circumstances. Be open to feedback and continuously seek ways to improve the performance management process. By effectively implementing performance management strategies, businesses can create a culture of high performance, engagement, and continuous improvement. This leads to increased productivity, employee satisfaction, and overall organizational success. Remember that performance management is an ongoing process that requires regular attention, communication, and commitment from all stakeholders involved.

Chapter 77: The Law of Employee Motivation

Employee motivation is crucial for the success of any business. When employees are motivated, they are more engaged, productive, and committed to their work. Understanding the Law of Employee Motivation can help business owners create a positive work environment and inspire their employees to excel.

THE IMPORTANCE OF EMPLOYEE MOTIVATION

Motivated employees play a significant role in driving business success. They are more likely to go above and beyond their job requirements, contribute innovative ideas, and deliver exceptional results. Motivated employees are also more likely to stay with a company long-term, reducing employee turnover and associated costs. When employees are motivated, they are more productive and efficient in their work. Motivated employees take ownership of their responsibilities and proactively seek opportunities to improve their performance. Employee motivation is closely linked to employee satisfaction and well-being. When employees feel motivated, they experience higher job satisfaction, leading to greater commitment and loyalty to the organization. Moreover, motivated employees create a positive work environment. They inspire and motivate their colleagues, fostering a culture of high performance and teamwork.

STRATEGIES FOR EMPLOYEE MOTIVATION

1. Clear Goals and Expectations: Set clear and achievable goals for your employees. Clearly communicate their roles and responsibilities, as well as the expectations you have for their performance. 2. Recognition and Rewards: Recognize and reward employees for their accomplishments and contributions. This could include

verbal praise, bonuses, promotions, or other forms of recognition that align with their preferences and values. 3. Professional Development Opportunities: Provide opportunities for employees to develop their skills and advance in their careers. Offer training programs, workshops, conferences, and mentorship opportunities to support their growth. 4. Employee Empowerment: Empower employees by delegating authority and decision-making power. Encourage them to take ownership of their work and provide them with autonomy to make decisions related to their responsibilities. 5. Communication and Feedback: Foster open and transparent communication with your employees. Provide regular feedback regarding their performance, acknowledging their strengths and areas for improvement. Encourage them to share their ideas and concerns. 6. Employee Well-being: Prioritize employee well-being by promoting work-life balance, offering flexible schedules, and providing resources for managing stress. Employee assistance programs and wellness initiatives can also contribute to their overall well-being. 7. Team Building Activities: Organize team-building activities to strengthen relationships and foster a sense of unity within the team. These activities can include team-building exercises, retreats, or social events. 8. Growth Opportunities: Offer opportunities for professional growth and advancement within the company. Promote from within whenever possible, as this demonstrates to employees that their hard work and dedication can lead to advancement. 9. Positive Work Environment: Create a positive and inclusive work environment where employees feel valued, respected, and supported. Encourage collaboration and celebrate diversity. 10. Purpose and Meaning: Help employees understand the purpose and meaning behind their work. Connect their individual tasks to the broader goals and mission of the organization. Show them how their contributions make a difference.

CONCLUSION

The Law of Employee Motivation highlights the importance of inspiring and engaging employees to achieve their full potential. By implementing strategies to motivate employees, businesses can create a positive work environment, enhance productivity, and achieve long-term success. Remember that every employee is unique, so it is essential to understand their individual needs and motivators to tailor your approach effectively.

Chapter 78: The Rule of Change Management

Change is inevitable in the business world. Industries evolve, technology advances, and customer demands shift. In order to thrive in this dynamic environment, businesses must effectively manage and adapt to change. The Rule of Change Management emphasizes the importance of embracing change and implementing strategies to navigate transitions successfully.

THE IMPORTANCE OF CHANGE MANAGEMENT

Change management is the process of planning, implementing, and controlling changes within an organization. It involves understanding the reasons behind the change, identifying the impact on various stakeholders, and developing strategies to minimize resistance and ensure a smooth transition. Change management is essential for several reasons: 1. **Adapting to Market Demands:** Business landscapes are continuously evolving, and organizations must stay agile and adaptable to remain competitive. Change management allows businesses to respond to market trends and customer demands efficiently. 2. **Increasing Efficiency:** Change often involves implementing new technologies, processes, or systems, which can improve operational efficiency and productivity. Effective change management ensures a seamless transition and minimizes disruptions to business operations. 3. **Driving Innovation:** Change can be a catalyst for innovation. By embracing change and encouraging a culture of innovation, businesses can identify new opportunities, develop creative solutions, and stay ahead of the competition. 4. **Managing Risks:** Change can introduce risks and uncertainties. Change management helps organizations identify and manage these risks effectively, mitigating potential negative impacts on the business. 5. **Enhancing Employee Engagement:** Change can create uncertainty and resistance among employees. By effectively managing change, organizations can engage and involve employees in the process, promoting a sense of ownership and commitment.

STRATEGIES FOR CHANGE MANAGEMENT

Implementing successful change management requires careful planning and execution. Here are some strategies to effectively manage change within an organization: 1. **Develop a Clear Change Vision:** Clearly communicate the reasons behind the change and the desired outcomes. Creating a compelling vision helps employees understand the need for change and align their efforts towards the common goal. 2. **Communicate Effectively:** Communication is essential throughout the change management process. Develop a communication plan that includes regular updates, clear instructions, and opportunities for employees to ask questions and provide feedback. Transparent communication helps minimize uncertainty and resistance. 3. **Provide Training and Support:** Equip employees with the necessary skills and knowledge to adapt to the change. Offer training programs, workshops, and resources to help employees understand and embrace new processes or technologies. Providing ongoing support ensures a successful transition. 4. **Involve Employees:** Engage employees in the change management process by seeking their input and involving them in decision-making. Creating cross-functional teams and task forces allows employees to contribute their expertise and insights. This involvement builds a sense of ownership and commitment to the change. 5. **Manage Resistance:** Resistance to change is natural, so it's essential to address it proactively. Identify potential barriers or challenges and develop strategies to overcome them. Addressing concerns, providing support, and highlighting the benefits of the change can help minimize resistance. 6. **Monitor and Evaluate:** Continuously monitor the progress of the change initiative and evaluate its impact on the organization. Collect feedback from employees and stakeholders, and make adjustments as needed. Regular evaluation ensures that the change is achieving the desired outcomes. 7. **Lead by Example:** Effective change management requires strong leadership. Leaders must demonstrate their commitment to the change, embrace the new processes or technologies, and inspire their teams to adapt. Leading by example sets the tone for the organization and encourages others to embrace the change.

THE BENEFITS OF EFFECTIVE CHANGE MANAGEMENT

Implementing effective change management strategies can bring several benefits to an organization, including: 1. **Smooth Transition:** Effective change management ensures a smooth transition from the old to the new, minimizing disruptions to business operations. 2. **Minimized Resistance:** By involving employees in the change process and addressing their concerns, resistance to change can be minimized. 3. **Increased Employee Engagement:** When employees are involved in the change process, they feel valued and engaged, leading to increased job satisfaction and productivity. 4. **Improved Efficiency and Productivity:** Change often introduces new processes or technologies that can streamline operations and improve efficiency. 5. **Innovation and Adaptability:** Effective change management fosters a culture of innovation and adaptability, positioning the organization for long-term success in a rapidly changing business landscape. 6. **Competitive Advantage:** Organizations that effectively manage change are better equipped to adapt to market trends and customer demands, giving them a competitive edge. By embracing the Rule of Change Management and implementing these strategies, businesses can navigate change successfully and position themselves for long-term success. Change becomes an opportunity for growth, innovation, and achieving strategic objectives.

Chapter 79: The Law of Crisis Management

Crisis management is a crucial aspect of business operations, as it involves handling unexpected events or emergencies that can potentially harm the organization's reputation, finances, or overall operations. The Law of Crisis Management emphasizes the importance of being prepared, proactive, and effective in responding to crises to minimize their impact and ensure business continuity.

THE IMPORTANCE OF CRISIS MANAGEMENT

Crisis management is not just about reacting to emergencies; it is about being prepared and developing robust strategies to handle crises in a calm and effective manner. The key reasons why crisis management is crucial for businesses include: 1. Protecting Reputation: Crises can damage a company's reputation, which is one of its most valuable assets. Implementing effective crisis management strategies helps protect the reputation and maintain public trust even in the face of adversity. 2. Minimizing Financial Impact: Crises can have significant financial consequences for businesses. By having a solid crisis management plan in place, companies can minimize the financial impact and recover more quickly. 3. Ensuring Business Continuity: Crises can disrupt normal business operations, leading to potential loss of revenue and customer dissatisfaction. Through effective crisis management, companies can ensure continuity and mitigate the negative effects on day-to-day operations.

KEY PRINCIPLES OF CRISIS MANAGEMENT

To effectively manage crises, businesses should adhere to several key principles: 1. Preparedness: Being prepared is essential to effectively manage crises. This involves conducting risk assessments, developing crisis management plans, and establishing communication channels and protocols. 2. Rapid Response: Quick response is crucial during a crisis. Having a designated crisis management team and clear lines of communication ensure that responses can be coordinated and executed promptly. 3. Communication: Open and transparent communication is vital during a crisis. Communicating with stakeholders, including employees, customers, shareholders, and the media, helps manage expectations, provide relevant updates, and address concerns. 4. Adaptability: Crises are often unpredictable, and circumstances can change rapidly. Being adaptable and flexible in response strategies is key to successfully managing crises. 5. Learning and Improvement: After a crisis, it is essential to conduct a thorough analysis of what went wrong and what could be improved. This involves evaluating response strategies, identifying lessons learned, and implementing changes to strengthen crisis management processes.

STRATEGIES FOR EFFECTIVE CRISIS MANAGEMENT

To effectively manage crises, businesses should implement several key strategies: 1. Develop a Crisis Management Plan: Create a detailed plan that outlines roles and responsibilities, communication protocols, and steps for handling different types of crises. 2. Conduct Risk Assessments: Identify potential risks and vulnerabilities to proactively address them before they escalate into crises. This includes assessing internal and external threats and developing contingency plans. 3. Establish Emergency Communication Protocols: Implement a robust communication system that includes clear lines of communication, designated spokespersons, and methods for disseminating timely and accurate information to stakeholders. 4. Train and Educate Employees: Provide comprehensive training to employees on crisis management procedures, including how to respond in various situations. This helps ensure that everyone is familiar with their roles and responsibilities during a crisis. 5. Regularly Review and Update the Crisis Management Plan: Regularly revisit and update the crisis management plan to reflect changes in the business environment, industry standards, or company structure. Conduct drills and simulations to test the effectiveness of the plan. 6. Maintain Relationships with Key Stakeholders: Build strong relationships with key stakeholders, including the media, government agencies, and industry associations. These relationships can be instrumental in crisis situations, as they can provide support, resources, and guidance. 7. Monitor and Analyze Social Media: In today's digital age, social media plays a critical role in shaping public perception during a crisis. Monitor social media channels, respond to inquiries and concerns, and address misinformation promptly. 8. Maintain Transparency and Honesty: During a crisis, it is crucial to remain transparent and honest in all communications. Avoid withholding information or providing false or misleading statements, as this can further damage the company's reputation.

CONCLUSION

The Law of Crisis Management emphasizes the importance of being prepared and proactive in handling crises. By developing comprehensive crisis management plans, implementing effective communication strategies, and continuously learning and improving, businesses can significantly minimize the impact of a crisis. Ultimately, effective crisis management helps protect the company's reputation, ensure business continuity, and strengthen relationships with stakeholders.

Chapter 80: The Rule of Customer Loyalty

In today's highly competitive business landscape, customer loyalty is more important than ever. The Rule of Customer Loyalty emphasizes the value of building long-term relationships with customers and creating a loyal customer base. When customers remain loyal to a business, they not only continue to purchase products or services, but they also become advocates, recommending the business to others and contributing to its growth and success. Customer loyalty goes beyond customer satisfaction. It is about creating an emotional connection with customers, meeting their needs and expectations consistently, and providing exceptional experiences that keep them coming back for more. Loyal customers are more likely to forgive occasional mistakes and setbacks, as they trust and value the relationship with the business. So, how can businesses foster customer loyalty? Here are some key strategies and principles to apply:

1. DELIVERING EXCEPTIONAL CUSTOMER SERVICE

One of the most important factors in building customer loyalty is providing exceptional customer service. This involves going above and beyond to meet and exceed customer expectations. When customers receive outstanding service, they feel appreciated and valued, which strengthens their loyalty to the business. Training employees to deliver top-notch service, responding promptly to customer inquiries and concerns, and addressing issues with empathy and professionalism are all crucial in building customer loyalty.

2. BUILDING STRONG RELATIONSHIPS

Building strong relationships with customers is essential for cultivating loyalty. This involves understanding their needs and preferences, personalizing interactions, and maintaining open and transparent communication. By treating customers as individuals and establishing a genuine connection, businesses can create a bond that goes beyond a simple transactional relationship. Regularly engaging with customers, seeking their feedback, and demonstrating that their opinion matters also contribute to building strong relationships and fostering loyalty.

3. OFFERING LOYALTY PROGRAMS AND INCENTIVES

Implementing loyalty programs and incentives can be effective in encouraging repeat business and increasing customer loyalty. Rewarding customers for their loyalty, such as offering exclusive discounts, early access to new products or services, or special perks, can create a sense of value and appreciation. Loyalty programs can also provide valuable data and insights into customer behavior, helping businesses tailor their offerings and communications to better serve their loyal customers.

4. PROVIDING CONSISTENT AND RELIABLE EXPERIENCES

Consistency is key in fostering customer loyalty. Customers appreciate businesses that consistently deliver on their promises, provide high-quality products or services, and offer a consistent level of customer experience. Maintaining consistency across all touchpoints, from initial contact to post-sales support, helps build trust and reliability, which are essential in nurturing customer loyalty.

5. ACTIVELY LISTENING AND ACTING ON CUSTOMER FEEDBACK

Listening to customer feedback and taking action based on their input is essential for building loyalty. Customers appreciate when businesses actively seek their opinions, take their feedback into consideration, and make improvements based on their suggestions. Actively listening to customers demonstrates that their voice matters and that the business is committed to continuously improving to better meet their needs.

6. GOING THE EXTRA MILE

To truly stand out and foster customer loyalty, businesses should be willing to go the extra mile. This can involve surprising and delighting customers with unexpected extras, personalized gestures, or exceptional service. Small acts of generosity and thoughtfulness can leave a lasting impression on customers and make them feel valued and appreciated. By following the Rule of Customer Loyalty and implementing these key strategies, businesses can build strong and loyal customer relationships. Loyal customers not only provide repeat business, but they also become brand advocates, referring others and helping to attract new customers. Cultivating loyalty leads to increased customer lifetime value, enhanced brand reputation, and long-term success in today's competitive marketplace.

www.ingramcontent.com/pod-product-compliance
Lightning Source LLC
Chambersburg PA
CBHW030421290526
45786CB00001B/74